D0597454

Dreams

Dreams

Discover the meanings of your nightly journeys

Pamela Ball

All images courtesy of Shutterstock.

ISBN: 978-1-83940-194-7
AD010179US

Printed in China

2 4 6 8 10 9 7 5 3 1

Contents

INTRODUCTION

The Penguin Dictionary of Psychology defines a dream in the following way: "A train of hallucinatory experiences with a certain degree of coherence, but often confused and bizarre, taking place in the condition of sleep and similar conditions."

SLEEPING AND DREAMING

Dreams are said to be the mind's way of making sense of the various types of input with which it has to cope. It has certainly been proved that human beings need sleep in order to function successfully and that the role of dreams seems to be balancing the psychological and physiological activity within us.

In the waking state we are continually feeding information into our brain, which is not filed in any efficient way. Dreams are therefore believed by many to perform two functions. One is the sorting and filing of the information. And the second is the presentation—in dreams—of all the information needed at any given time for dreamers to interact more wholly with the world in which they live.

When the limitations that the conscious mind places on the thought processes are removed, the mind is free to roam wherever it pleases—in dream realities. Free of inhibition, it creates scenarios that often defy explanation by the logical side of the personality. In looking for explanations of these dreams, we have to become more instinctive and creative in our pursuit of knowledge, which opens up ways of approaching things that often would have seemed impossible on a conscious level.

During this process, we tap into not only our *own* storehouse of memories, perceptions, beliefs and images, but also into an even more subtle level of information that is available to everyone. This is the level that Jung labeled the "collective unconscious"—a collection of inherited norms of conduct, beliefs, ideals and related symbols that repeatedly emerge in us all.

A BRIEF HISTORY OF DREAMS

Dream interpretation has a long, checkered history. Ancient peoples had great faith in prophetic dreams, which they called visions. They believed that they were sent by the gods as warnings and guidance. In the light of the modern-day belief that many dreams come from the Higher Self, or more spiritual side of ourselves, we have come almost full circle.

By the 4th century AD, dreams were considered important enough for a seer called Artemidorus to have put on record "The Five Books of Dream Interpretation." Until the 19th century, when Freud began to look at dreams, many of the interpretations that Artemidorus gave were accepted as accurate. Indeed, many books on dream interpretation still hold traces of his interpretations.

The early psychoanalysts, particularly Freud, believed that dreams could be explained according to our attitude to our own sex and sexuality. As more information became available to therapists and dream workers through research, it became apparent that this was not the only basis for explanation.

Therapists such as Freud believed that it was only possible to decode dreams with professional help. However, we now know that this is untrue—unless the dreamer is receiving medication for depression or some such difficulty.

As Freud's students realized that it wasn't wise to give the analysts all the power, especially because of how colored the interpretations could become by the unconscious perceptions of the analysts

Sigmund Freud believed that our dreams held clues to our attitudes toward sex and sexuality—clues that could help an analyst unlock our deepest, subconscious desires.

themselves, a movement rose to widen the interpretation of dreams. Jung, having been a student of Freud, suggested that one way to interpret them was to recognize dream elements and characters as part of the dreamer's own personality. This kind of subjective approach was greatly liberating, putting the interpretive power back in the hands of dreamers who are, after all, the only ones with access to the inner recesses of their own minds.

It was from this that Jung's renowned work on the Archetypes arose, although we don't cover them in detail in this book because it's so well covered elsewhere. He recognized the validity of the sexual impulse arising from the duality of the masculine and feminine. In so doing, he accepted that there were certain unacknowledged inner parts of ourselves—such as our Shadow (the neglected side of each individual), the Anima (the inner feminine in men) and the Animus (the inner masculine in women)—that dreams could sometimes reveal to us, as well as the more *obvious* dream interpretations.

Later significant dream work was done principally by Calvin Hall—who came to view dreams as a kind of personal document that gave symbolic clues as to the psyche of the individual—and Fritz Perls, who developed the Gestalt theory, viewing dreams as the road to wholeness, allowing us to reclaim parts of our personalities that had become lost.

THE AIM OF THIS BOOK

This book attempts to draw all the strands of dream interpretation together so that you, the dreamer, can develop to your highest potential. It has been designed to enable you to begin your *own* journey of dream exploration—and become your *own* dream therapist.

With the help of the information about dream symbols in the pages that follow, *you* will get to decide what your dreams mean and what you are going to do about them. And, above all, *you* will get to decide to what degree you will allow your dreams to affect your everyday life and vice versa.

Starting on page 12 is a dictionary of symbols—presented in alphabetical order for your ease of use. You will see that some entries, such as Animal and House, have various sub-categories within them to help you dive deeper with your interpretations.

Keeping a Dream Diary

To get the best from the book, it is best to record your dreams—preferably in a dream diary—as soon as you can after they happen.

This can be done by recording your voice or writing down everything you can remember as soon as you wake up: the setting of the dream, what all the images were, who was present, what was said or done, what you as the dreamer felt about it, what emotions were present, and how everything hung together.

You might find it helpful to order each key symbol that you remember in alphabetical order—for ease of use with the book entries.

Then simply look up each symbol in the pages that follow and decide which of the interpretations most resonate with you. By doing this, you will be able to more fully understand the emotional content and the reason for each particular dream that you have.

Gaining Further Insight

You will sometimes have immediate insights and clarifications that will be enough to allow you to interpret your dreams successfully. However, there may often be many interpretations of the same dream that are equally valid.

One of the most effective ways of gaining further insight if a dream is difficult to interpret is to work with a supportive friend. Often by talking about the dream with another person, you will remember additional aspects or see things in a different light, which enables enhanced interpretation. Additionally, some interaction between dream characters may become obvious, which might offer new insights. However, it is crucial that the supporting friends ask only questions that clarify your dream, rather than asking leading questions.

A useful approach can be to explore the dream first from the dreamer's personal point of view (e.g. "I was...", "We were...", "I seemed..."), and then to work more objectively with the images (e.g. "The room was in a large house," "The tree was very odd…"), allowing the dreamer's perspective to shift to that of an observer.

It can then be useful for the dreamer to choose one of the characters or images in the dream, to "become" that character or object, and to experience the dream from that viewpoint. Since all the parts of our dreams are aspects of ourselves (even objects such as cars and trees), by experiencing the scenario from a different perspective, we gain additional insight into ourselves. This process can be continued with each image in the dream until you feel that you have a better understanding. With practice, you will become more proficient at interpreting your own symbols.

ROAD MAP FOR YOUR DREAM EXPLORATIONS

Regularly working with your dreams in the ways just outlined—whether positive dreams, anxiety dreams, magical dreams, nightmares or any other type—will allow you to gradually learn more about yourself and your private dream world.

The premise is that the better you understand yourself and the world in which you live, the happier, more fulfilled, and more enriched your future will be for both yourself and those in the wider world around you. So we hope you enjoy the explorations that this dream road map allow to unfold…

THE DREAMER'S DICTIONARY

AN A-Z OF DREAM SYMBOLS

A: Abandoned to Axe

ABANDONED Similar to the sense of being rejected, this represents a sense of how we experienced not being wanted when we were young. This may not actually be how it was, but our feelings give us that perception. For instance, a child having had to go into the hospital may have recurring dreams in adulthood of being abandoned, and may have problems forming plans for future success.

ABROAD To dream about **being or going abroad** gives us an understanding of our feelings toward the widening of our horizons, or making changes in our life. Such dreams may also be connected to beliefs about the country in the dream. We are dreaming about personal freedom or the ability to move freely around our universe.

ABSENCE A dream about someone being absent, or of the absence of something that one would expect to find, indicates that the unexpected may happen. We may be looking for something that we have already lost. Our feelings about the absence (e.g. fear or anger) may also be important. A child experiences a strong sense of loss when his or her mother is first absent from his or her perceived environment, and this can cause extreme distress.

ABSORB To be **absorbed in what we are doing** in dreams indicates our ability to be totally focused on our action. We are capable of taking in ideas or beliefs, which then become part of us and the way we function. To **absorb something into ourselves** is to consume it, in the sense of making it our own. A great deal of the process of understanding takes place through absorption of information.

ABYSS—*also see Pit* To dream about an abyss indicates that the dreamer recognizes within themselves the so-called bottomless pit or void. This is an aspect of the unknown that all of us must face at some time or another in our life. It is a risky action that must be taken with faith and courage.

ACCIDENT Dreams of being injured, murdered or killed occur relatively frequently, and attention needs to be paid to the specific circumstances of the dream. We are usually receiving a warning to be careful or to be aware of hidden aggression, either our own or others'.

ACID There is a corrosive influence in the dreamer's life that is usually bad but may be cleansing. There could be the feeling that the dreamer is being eaten away by some action or concept. The necessity is to become aware of something that must be used with caution, depending how, and on whom, it is being used.

ACORN To dream about acorns indicates that there is a huge growth process beginning to emerge from small beginnings. There is a new potential for strength. Since acorns appear in autumn, there may be a need to harvest or gather up the ideas before they can be stored in order to give them time to work.

ACTION The action in a dream often informs the dreamer of hidden agendas and motivations, since each of us is the producer of our own lives. What we—or others—are doing in a dream often needs to be interpreted as much as the articles in the dream.

ACTOR To dream about an actor, particularly **a famous one**, is to become aware of the ego in oneself. Very often we become conscious of the roles we play in life, and recognize that we are perhaps not playing the part we really want to.

ADDICTION To dream about **being addicted** indicates that we have to recognize that there is a need and desire to acknowledge obsessive behavior in ourselves or others. There is anxiety that someone or something is taking us over. To **be addicted to someone** is to have abdicated responsibility for ourselves. To **be addicted to a substance** such as tobacco or alcohol in a dream suggests an inability to relate properly to the world in which we live.

ADVERTISEMENT Depending on the content of the dream, this indicates areas in our life that need to be acknowledged or recognized. For instance, **an advertisement on a billboard** might mean a way of working in the world, whereas a **television ad** might represent a way of thinking.

AFFAIR Dreaming about an affair allows us to come to terms with our sexual needs and desires for excitement and stimulation. We may feel the need to do something naughty or something that means we have to take emotional risks.

AIRPLANE Dreams of airplanes can represent sudden or dramatic life changes. **An airplane taking off** represents a leap into the unknown and taking risks. **An airplane landing** indicates the success of a new venture or the outcome of a calculated risk.

AIRPORT In dreaming about an airport we are entering a stage of transition, making decisions to move into new areas of life. It may also indicate we are, or should be, making a fresh assessment of our own identity.

ALCOHOL—*also see Drunk, Intoxication and Wine* When alcohol appears in a dream, we may be in need of a pleasurable experience or influence. We have available means of changing perception. We can afford to let go and go "with the flow" of what is happening to us.

ALIEN If we dream about an alien, there is perhaps something unknown and frightening, which needs to be faced. We have never encountered the strangeness of the being that appears in our dream, and we must handle whatever happens.

ALONE Dreaming about **being alone** highlights being single, isolated or lonely. More positively, it represents the need for independence. Loneliness can be experienced as a negative state, whereas being alone can be very positive. Often in dreams, a feeling is highlighted in order for us to recognize whether it is positive or negative.

ALTAR—*also see Table* An altar in a dream represents the means or need to give oneself up to something that is more important than the immediate situation. Usually an altar represents religious belief of some kind. It is the table of communion—togetherness—but also it often suggests the division between the physical and the spiritual.

AMNESIA To suffer from amnesia in a dream indicates our attempts to blot out the disliked. It also indicates a fear of change. Losing one's memory in real life can be traumatic, but in dreams it can be even more of a problem since we do not know how much we actually should remember. We do not know how much is viable, and how much is presented for the purposes of that dream only.

AMPUTATION When we dream about **amputation of one of our limbs**, it can mean that we fear or risk losing a part of ourselves that we value. To dream about **amputating someone else's limb** indicates our ability to deny others their right to self-expression.

ANESTHETIC To be anesthetized in a dream indicates that we are trying to avoid painful emotions, and that we are feeling overpowered by external circumstances. It may even indicate that we are being forced to avoid something.

ANALYST Whatever kind of analyst we dream about, it's a reminder that we have inside ourselves a monitor that alerts us to the need to analyze our actions and reactions. We should exercise self-awareness and analyze our life, breaking it down into manageable parts.

ANCHOR When an anchor appears in a dream, it can generally be taken to mean the necessity to remain stable in emotional situations. We need to grasp an idea that will give us a point of reference in difficult situations.

ANGEL Dreaming about angels indicates that we are searching for a parental figure who gives unconditional love and support, or that we need to develop these qualities ourselves. We may be trying to introduce religious concepts into our life.

ANGER Anger in a dream can often represent other passionate emotions. We may, for example, be struggling with how to appropriately express something that is distressing us in waking life, so it comes out in dreams instead.

ANIMALS When animals appear in a dream, they usually represent an aspect of the personality that cannot be correctly understood except on an instinctive level.

Animal with a cub This will represent motherly qualities and therefore is a symbol for the mother.

Baby animals The dreamer will be dealing with the childlike side of their personality, or possibly children known to them.

Hurt young animal The dreamer may perceive a difficulty in becoming mature or facing life.

Eating an animal The dream could be about the "demons" one creates, which can only be overcome by assimilating them in a constructive way. In Pagan belief, it was thought that we would take on certain superior aspects of any animal that we ate.

God-like, talking, awe-inspiring or wise animals, or those with human characteristics Animals have not yet become conscious of, or pitted themselves against, the power from which they came, so the wisdom they show is innocent and simple. It is always important to pay attention to this aspect of animal life in dreams, since we need to be in touch with that part of ourselves.

Helpful animals The subconscious is producing helpful images from its depths. The figures of animals are an easy way for the dreamer to accept that help.

Killing an animal This may destroy the energy derived from the instincts.

Taming or harnessing an animal This shows the efforts made to control the dreamer's instincts and, if possible, make them productive and useful.

Trying to find some refuge from animals Whether by building defenses or by running away, this is indicative of the dreamer's struggle with his own animal instincts, and whether the action being taken is adequate. Such instincts may be threatening or damaging to aspects of the dreamer's life.

ANTLERS—*also see Horns* The deer is a noble animal, so the interpretation differs if the antlers are **mounted, as in a trophy**, or are seen **on the animal**. If the latter, then the interpretation is that of something supernormal, and may represent intellectual powers. If the former, then antlers may be interpreted as attempting to achieve high status.

APPLE—*also see Food and Fruit* In dreams, this often represents fruitfulness, love and/or temptation.

APPETITE When an appetite is particularly noticeable in a dream, it usually represents a desire that is unfulfilled. This could be a physical desire, an emotional one, or a spiritual one.

APPOINTMENT Dreaming about **going to an appointment** indicates that we need to have an aim or a goal. **Missing an appointment** suggests that we are not paying enough attention to detail.

ARC Dreaming about an arc shape is often a sign that we need to concentrate on a particular part of our life.

ARCH When we dream about arches or doorways, we are often moving into a different environment or way of life. We have to go through some form of initiation or acceptance ritual in order to succeed.

ARENA Dreaming about being **in an arena, either as a player or as a spectator**, highlights the fact that we may need to make a decision to move into a specifically created environment, one that gives us more room for self-expression and creativity or theatricality.

ARMS—*also see Body and Weapons* We use our arms in all kinds of different ways, and in dreams it is often significant to note what is actually taking place. We may be defending ourselves, fighting, being held, or acknowledging, for example.

ARMOR If we dream about armor, we may need to be aware of emotional and intellectual rigidity in either ourselves or the people around us. If ***we* are in armor**, we may be overprotecting ourselves, whereas if ***others* are in armor**, we may be overly aware of their defense mechanisms.

ARRESTED To dream about **being arrested** suggests the restraint of one's natural self-expression by moral judgments or questions of right or wrong from other people. To dream about **arresting someone else** would indicate our instinctive disapproval of the part of ourselves that is represented by that person in the dream.

ARROW—*also see Weapons* If we dream about **shooting arrows**, we are aware of the consequences of actions, either our own or other people's, which cannot be recalled or revoked. Interestingly enough, arrows can also symbolize words in dreams.

ARTIST An artist in a dream encourages us to recognize the artist within ourselves—the aspect of ourselves that is in contact with the creative side of the unconscious.

ASCENSION / ASCENDING If we feel ourselves ascending in a dream, we may be becoming conscious of being able to exercise control over passion or sexual pleasure, or it may represent a breakthrough to a new spiritual plane that transcends the state of being human. It is an awareness of different levels of concentration that give a different perspective to being human.

ASCETIC To **meet an ascetic or holy man** in a dream is to meet our higher self, and to recognize the part of ourselves that is continually seeking unity with the divine. There may be some conflict with natural drives, we may be looking for simplicity, or there may be an avoidance of sex or contact as a result of fear or the need for restraint.

ASHES Ashes in a dream often indicate penitence and sorrow. We are aware that we have been overanxious or foolish in a particular situation, and that there is little left to be done because the situation has outlived its usefulness. After an event or person has gone, we may dream about a fire that has died down, leaving ashes. These are what remains of our experience, which will enable us to make the most of our current situation.

ATTACK **Being attacked** in a dream indicates a fear of being under threat from external events or internal emotions. Unknown impulses or ideas force the dreamer into taking a defensive attitude. If we are **being attacked by animals**, we are turning our own aggression and/or sexuality inwards; we have fear of our own natural urges.

AUDIENCE If we are standing in **front of an audience** in a dream, we probably have to deal with an important issue in our life. If we are **in the audience**, we are witnessing an emotion or process of change in ourselves.

AVALANCHE If we **witness an avalanche** in our dreams, we are experiencing a destructive force. If we are **in the middle of an avalanche**, we are being overwhelmed by circumstances.

AX—*also see Weapons* When we dream about an ax, we need to figure out whether it is being **used against us**, or we **are using** it. If it is being used against us, we feel that we are being threatened by someone's greater power, whereas using **an ax** indicates that we need to become aware of the destructive forces within ourselves.

B: Back to Butterfly

BACK—*also see Body* Dreaming about **seeing someone's back** suggests that we should identify the more private elements in our character. We might also find that we are vulnerable to the unexpected. If we dream about **turning our back on something**, we are rejecting the feeling being experienced in the dream.

BACKBONE / SPINE—*also see Body* If the backbone is particularly noticeable in a dream, we need to consider our main support structure.

BACKWARDS To dream about going backwards indicates that we may be withdrawing from a situation or slow to learn from it. We may need to recognize that to continue in a particular situation will stop our progress.

BAD When we dream about something being "bad," we are being made aware that the dream object is now worthless or defective. **Feeling bad** can have two meanings: one in the sense of **being naughty**, and the other **not feeling right**.

In both cases, we find that we are off balance in some way and the dream is drawing our attention to this fact.

BAG A bag in a dream may mean that we are having problems with the feminine elements in our identity. Depending on the type of bag (e.g. **a handbag or a shopping bag**), we may be hiding certain aspects of ourselves from public consideration.

BAGGAGE To be carrying **extra baggage** in a dream means that we may be carrying an extra load, either emotional or practical. We may be expecting too much of ourselves or of others. We are carrying past hurt or trauma.

BAIT Dreaming about putting out bait can be an indication of doubts about our own ability to attract a partner. We may feel that we have to entrap a partner.

BAKER—*also see Oven* Dreaming about a baker alerts us to the ability that we all have to alter our approach or attitude to situations in our life.

BALANCE When we dream about trying to **maintain our balance**, or being **balanced in a difficult position**, we are searching for equilibrium. To dream about searching for the **balance in a financial account** means we are looking for something that, at present, remains unrecognized and unknown.

BALD To dream about **someone who is bald** indicates we are being made aware of a degree of dullness in our life.

BALL A ball connects with the playful, childlike side of ourselves and our need to express ourselves with freedom. **Attending a ball** (as in a dance) also suggests a need for freedom, but links with the more flamboyant side of ourselves.

BALLERINA—*also see Dance* The fairy-like appearance of the ballerina in a dream shows that we are making a connection with that side of our being. We may also be searching for balance and poise.

BALLOON Very often it is the color of balloons in our dreams that are important *(see Color)*. However, they can also indicate a party mood or a desire for sex.

BAMBOO The pliability of bamboo indicates yielding but enduring strength. As one of the most graceful but hardy of plants, it also represents these qualities in the dreamer—or that they should try to develop these attributes.

BANANA—*also see Food and Fruit* Most dreams about fruit have to do with sexuality or sensuality. Conventionally, the banana, because of its shape, signifies the penis. However, it is also considered, because of its yielding nature, to represent the handling of masculine sexuality.

BAND If the dreamer sees a **band or stripe** of color, for example, there may be some limitation in their circumstances that needs to be recognized. If, however, the image is of a **band of musicians**, this would indicate the need for teamwork.

BANDAGE If a **bandage is being applied** in a dream it shows the beginning of a healing process. There may be hurt feelings or emotional injuries that need attention.

BANK A bank appearing in a dream may mean that the financial, mental or spiritual resources of the dreamer need careful management. The sense of security, without which we cannot venture into the world, needs to be correctly managed and monitored.

BANKER Money and personal resources are things with which many people have difficulty. Our need for an authority figure to help us deal with problems that arise is usually symbolized by the banker or bank manager in dreams.

BANQUET If we dream about **serving** at a banquet, we should be careful not to deny ourselves the good things in life by being too giving. If we are **attending** a banquet, we should recognize our need to be nurtured.

BAPTISM To dream about **being baptized** indicates a new influence entering the dreamer's life, cleansing away old attitudes and opening up to one's inner possibilities. To dream about **baptizing someone** means the dreamer is ready to pass on knowledge to other people.

BAR When we dream about a metal bar, such as an **iron bar**, we should look at how rigid or aggressive we are being in our behavior. We need to handle ourselves with strength of purpose. To be **in a bar** and aware of our behavior

indicates how we relate to groups and what our feelings are about society in general. We might feel that it's appropriate to use a public space to create new relationships, or to come to terms with our sense of loneliness.

BARBED WIRE To be surrounded by **barbed wire** in a dream indicates that we are being prevented from moving forward by either our own, or others', hurtful remarks.

BARE—*also see Naked and Nude* If the **dreamer is bare**, he or she is becoming aware of his or her vulnerability. If the **landscape is bare** there is a lack of happiness or perhaps of fertility.

BAREFOOT Depending on the circumstances of the dream, to be barefoot can indicate either poverty or the recognition of sensual freedom.

BASE If our attention is drawn to the **base of an object** we may need to go back to the starting point of a project in which we are involved in waking life. We should consider how stable we are in any situation.

BASKET To dream about a basket, particularly a full one, is to dream about fruition and abundance. It can also represent the feminine closing principle.

BAT—*also see Vampire* To dream about bats (the animal) indicates that there are thoughts and ideas in the unconscious that may reveal themselves with frightening potential. Dreaming about a **baseball bat** or other type of sports bat will give an indication of our attitude toward controlled aggression, or of how we deal with external forces.

BATHTUB, BATHING Dreaming about **being in the bathtub** may indicate the need for cleansing some old feelings. We have an opportunity to contemplate what has occurred in the past and to adopt new attitudes.

BATON If the dream is of a **police baton**, it can represent authority.

BAY To dream about **a bay, seashore or inlet** shows we are aware of where we can be more receptive.

BEACH To be on a beach shows our awareness of the boundary between emotion and reality—our ability to be in touch with the elements.

BEACON This can show, variously, a warning, the need for communication, or a strongly held principle by which one lives.

BEADS—*also see Necklace* When we dream about beads—including in **a rosary**—we are making a connection with continuity. **To dream about beads breaking** indicates the failure of a favorite project.

BEAN To be **storing beans** in a dream may show a fear of failure or a lack of confidence in our ability to carry through an objective, and the need to create something in the future. **To be planting beans** would suggest faith in the future, and a wish to create something useful. Traditionally, the bean was supposed to be capable of feeding, clothing and providing an object of exchange for barter.

BEAR A **live bear** in a dream indicates aggression, whereas a **dead** one represents the handling of one's deeper negative instincts. To dream about a **toy bear**—i.e. a teddy bear—shows a childlike need for security.

BEARD To dream about a man with a beard means we must guard against cover-up and deceit.

BEATING The act of **beating something or someone** in a dream represents our need for power by aggression and brute force.

BED—*also see Furniture and Mattress* To be **going to bed alone** in a dream can indicate a desire for a return to the safety and security of the womb. To dream about a **bed made up with fresh linens** indicates the need for a fresh approach to the thoughts and ideas that really matter to us.

BEE As a symbol of something to be feared, as well as tamed and used, the meaning of bees in dreams can be ambivalent. To be **stung by a bee** is a warning of the possibility of hurt.

BEEHIVE The beehive is said to represent an ordered community and therefore the ability to absorb chaos.

BEGGAR To dream about **being a beggar** represents our own feeling of failure and lack of self-esteem. To dream about **someone else as a beggar** indicates we need to become aware of our ability to help those who are less fortunate than us.

BEHAVIOR Our (or others') behavior in a dream can differ markedly from normal, since the dream state gives us the freedom to highlight aspects of ourselves of which we would not normally be aware.

BEHIND To be behind someone in a dream indicates that, on a subconscious level, we may consider ourselves to be inferior in some way.

BELL Traditionally, to **hear a bell tolling** in a dream was to be warned of disaster or death. While that meaning is less prevalent now, as there are more efficient ways of communication, a bell in a dream (such as a **doorbell**) does warn us to be on the alert. It may also indicate that we have a desire to communicate with someone who is distanced or estranged from us.

BELLY To be aware of **someone else's belly, or stomach**, in a dream draws our attention to their emotions.

BELT To dream about a belt that attracts our attention represents the fact that we are perhaps being bound by old attitudes, duty and so on. An **ornate belt** can represent a symbol of power or office (as in regimental or nurses' belts).

BIBLE—*also see Religious Imagery* If we dream about a Bible or other religious book, it usually means that we are aware of traditional morality.

BICYCLE—*also see Journey* To dream about **riding a bicycle** shows the need to pay attention to personal effort or motivation.

BIRDS Birds in dreams usually represent freedom, imagination, thoughts, and ideas that, by nature, need freedom to be able to become evident. Man has been fascinated by birds and flight since ancient times. Birds were believed to be vehicles for the soul and to be able to carry the soul to heaven. As a result, birds were very often invested with magical and mystical powers.

BIRTH We tend to dream about birth at the beginning of a new way of life, a new attitude, new ability, or new project—also when we become aware of the death of the old.

BITE Being bitten in a dream may show that we are experiencing aggression from someone, or that our own aggressive instincts are not under control.

BIZARRE Dream images are often bizarre in that someone may be doing something that is very odd, or something may have a strange or grotesque appearance. This is usually because it is important that we remember the image in order to understand.

BLINDFOLDING If we have **been blindfolded** in a dream, it shows that a deliberate attempt is being made to deceive us. If we are **blindfolding someone** else, perhaps we are not being entirely honest in our dealings with other people, even if through ignorance.

BLINDNESS If we are suffering from blindness in a dream, there is an inability or unwillingness to "see" something—possibly qualities in ourselves that we don't like.

BLOCK In dreams, a block may present itself in many forms. We can experience it as a physical block—that is, something that needs to be climbed over or gotten around, a mental block (such as not being able to speak or hear), or a spiritual block (such as an angel or demon appearing in our dreams).

BLOOD From time immemorial, blood has represented the life-carrier or the life force. To dream about a **violent scene where blood appears** indicates that we are being self-destructive in some way. If we are having to **deal with blood**, we need to be aware of our own strength. If we have been injured and **someone else is dealing with the blood**, we need to look at what help is necessary to overcome hurt.

BOAT / SHIP—*also see Journey* To dream about a boat or ship often indicates how we cope with our own emotions and those of others. It may represent how we navigate our way through life and whether we are in control of our life.

BODY The body represents the individual and is the outward physical manifestation of all that we are. Since being "physical" is a baby's first experience of itself, the body forms the prime source of information.

BONDS If we dream about savings **bonds** (promissory notes), it can indicate that we have a sense of commitment to a person or a principle, that we are capable of making promises that we can keep. If we dream about the kind of **bonds, bindings and cords** that can occur in relationships, whoever is being "bound" is showing submission to a greater force.

BONES Bones appearing in a dream usually indicate that we need to "go back to basics." To dream about a **dog eating a bone** means that we need to consider our basic instincts. To dream about **finding bones** indicates that there is something essential that we have not considered in a situation.

BOMB—*also see Nuclear Explosion* Bombs appearing in a dream usually indicate some form of explosive situation with which we need to deal. **Exploding** a bomb indicates the need for positive action, whereas **defusing** a bomb suggests being careful not to make a situation worse.

BOOK Our search for knowledge, and the ability to learn from other people's experience and opinions, is symbolized in dreams by books and libraries. To dream about **old books** represents inherited wisdom and spiritual awareness. To dream about **account books** indicates the need or ability to look after our own resources. To dream about a **novel** represents a different way of looking at things. For instance, a **historical novel** might suggest we need to explore the past, whereas a **romantic novel** would suggest the need to look at relationships.

BOUQUET **To be given** a bouquet in a dream shows that we recognize our own abilities but also expect others to recognize them. To be **giving someone else** a bouquet indicates that we fully recognize their positive qualities.

BORDER A border can appear in many different ways in a dream. To have our attention drawn to the **edge or border of material** can indicate changes that we will make in the material world. To be standing on **a border, or frontier, between two countries** can show the need to make great changes in life—perhaps physically moving our place of residence.

BOTTLE To a certain extent it depends on which type of bottle is perceived in the dream. **To see a baby bottle** would indicate the need to be successfully nurtured and helped to grow. **A bottle of alcohol** would show the need to celebrate, or to curb an excess, while **a medicine bottle** might symbolize the need to look at one's own health. **A broken bottle** could indicate either aggression or failure.

BOW Since bowing is indicative of giving someone else status, to be **bowing to someone in** a dream would indicate our sense of inferiority. To perceive a bow, as in **Cupid's bow**, in a dream can indicate the need to be loved—the union of masculine and feminine.

BOWL **A bowl of food** in a dream represents our ability to nurture and sustain others. **A bowl of flowers** can represent a gift or a talent, while a **bowl of water** represents our emotional capacity.

BOX **To feel boxed in** in a dream is to be prevented from expanding in an appropriate way. To dream about **packing things** in a box indicates that we are trying to get rid of feelings or thoughts with which we cannot cope.

BRAID In olden times, a **braid using three strands** indicated the interweaving of body, mind, and spirit. It also represented the influences that were assimilated by a growing girl and taken into her understanding of herself as a woman. In dreams, it therefore represents womanhood and femininity.

BRAIN When attention is drawn to the brain in a dream, we are expected to consider our own or others' intellect. To dream about the **brain being preserved** indicates the need to take care in intellectual pursuits. We may be pushing ourselves too hard.

BREAD—*also see Food* Dreaming about bread connects us with our need for basic emotional and biological satisfaction. To be **sharing bread** in a dream represents our ability to share basic experience.

BREAK To dream about something being broken symbolizes loss or damage. If a **favorite object** is broken, we must make changes and break from the past. If a **limb is broken** we may be prevented from moving forward or carrying out a certain action.

BREATH To become aware of **one's own breathing** in a dream indicates a deep connection with the process of life. To be aware of **someone else's breathing** indicates the need for empathy and understanding toward that person.

BREEZE To dream about a breeze being meaningful indicates a contented state of mind. Wind is usually considered to belong to the intellect, so, by association, a gentle breeze indicates love, while a strong breeze indicates a degree of abrasiveness.

BRIDE—*also see Marriage* When a woman **dreams of being a bride**, she is often trying to reconcile her need for a relationship and her need for independence. **In a man's dream**, a bride indicates his understanding of the feminine, innocent part of himself. To dream about **being at a wedding**, especially your own, indicates the integration of inner feeling and outer reality.

BRIDEGROOM—*also see Marriage* To dream about a bridegroom usually indicates the desire to be married or to find a partner. It often shows a desire to be more responsible or to take on responsibility for someone else. It is a connection to, and an understanding of, the "romantic" side of one's nature and indicates the need for integration of the intellect and the real world.

BRIDGE A bridge is one of the most commonly found images in dreams, and almost invariably indicates crossing from one phase of life to another. The bridge may be depicted as weak or strong, sturdy or otherwise, which gives an indication of the strength of connection necessary to make changes in the dreamer's life.

BRIGHT To experience brightness in a dream means that some part of our life needs illuminating, often by an external source.

BROADCAST When we dream about **taking part in a broadcast**, we are aware of needing to reach a wider audience. This may be risky since we have no means of measuring our audience's response. To dream about **listening to a broadcast** means that we should be listening to the message that other people are trying to get across.

BROTHERHOOD Dreaming about **belonging to a brotherhood** indicates our need to belong to a group of like-minded people.

BRUTALITY To experience some form of brutality in a dream can be frightening until we realize that we are connecting to the darker, more animal side of ourselves. We may need to deal with fears associated with that side in order to make progress.

BUBBLE We may dream about bubbles as part of our need to have fun in a childlike way. We often become aware of the temporary nature of happiness and our need for illusion.

BUCKLE Dreaming about an **ornate buckle** has the same symbolism as that of a belt in that it can represent the holding of high office or status. It can also indicate honor, and can be a symbol of loyalty or membership.

BUD To dream about a bud is to recognize the unfolding of a new way of life, new experiences, or new emotions. To dream about a **bud dying**, or shriveling up, indicates the failure of a project.

BUDDHA In dreams, the Buddha represents the denial or loss of ego—a sign that there needs to be a liberation from thinking and desiring.

BULL In dreams, a bull represents the masculine principle and fertility. It can also indicate the way we handle male sexuality.

BULLET To dream about bullets is to be aware of aggression and a desire to hurt. If the bullet is **being fired at** the dreamer, it may be considered a warning of danger. If, however, the dreamer is **firing the bullet,** there is an awareness of one's vulnerability.

BURGLAR When we become aware of a burglar or intruder in our dreams we are experiencing some form of violation of our private space. This may be from external sources or from inner fears and difficult emotions, and indicates that we are feeling threatened.

BURIAL To have a dream about **being buried** indicates a fear of being overcome, possibly by responsibility, or of repressing parts of our personality.

BUS—*also see Journey* If we dream about being **on a bus** we are coming to terms with the way we handle group relationships, and new directions we need to take in company with others.

BUTCHER We see the butcher as one who mutilates, but provides for us at the same time, and this is reflected in dreams when he or she appears as someone who separates the good from the bad. He or she may also be a destroyer.

BUTTERFLY On a practical level, when seen in dreams, the butterfly represents lightheartedness and freedom.

C: Cage to Crutch

CAGE / CELL—*also see Prison* The cage normally represents some form of trap or jail. To dream about **caging a wild animal** alerts us to our need to restrain our wilder instincts. To dream that we are **in a cage** indicates a sense of frustration and perhaps of being trapped by the past.

CAKES When we dream about a **celebration cake**—such as a wedding cake or a birthday cake—we are being shown that there is cause for celebration in our life. This may have to do with the actual cause for celebration or simply to mark the passage of time. (**Candles on a cake**— *see Candle.*)

CALENDAR If a calendar appears in a dream, our attention may be being drawn to the past, present, or future, and something significant in our life, or perhaps we're being warned about the passage of time in an important scheme.

CAMEL Depending on the environment in the dream, the camel can represent the unusual or bizarre. It also represents available resources and obedience to a basic principle.

CAMERA To be **using a camera** in a dream means that we are recording events that we may need to remember or take note of more fully. **Being filmed** indicates that we need to look more carefully at our actions and reactions to certain situations.

CANAL Because a canal is a man-made structure, a dream about a canal usually indicates that we are inclined to be rigid as far as the control of our emotions is concerned. We may be introducing too much structure into our life at the expense of our creativity.

CANCER Cancer is one of the prime fears a human being has to deal with, so to dream about cancer indicates that we may be somehow out of harmony with our body. It indicates fear of illness and can represent something "eating away" at us—usually a negative idea.

CANDLE In Pagan times, a candle represented the dispersing of darkness and a way of worshipping power. To dream about candles indicates that we are trying to clarify something we do not understand. **Candles on a birthday cake** indicate that we are marking a transition from the old to the new. **Lighting a candle** represents using courage and fortitude or asking for something we need.

CANE Because many people associate a cane with some form of punishment or sadism, it can represent self-punishment or masochism. Its appearance in a dream is more likely, however, to mean that we are trying to come to terms with some form of childhood trauma.

CANOE To dream about a canoe would indicate that we are handling our emotions in isolation—possibly trying to control their flow. We are aware that we are capable of making changes, but only by our own efforts.

CANOPY When we dream about a canopy we are looking to be protected, sheltered or loved. In olden times, a canopy was used to shelter those with special duties or powers, such as kings and queens or priests and priestesses. We still acknowledge this privilege on a deep internal level. If **we ourselves are being sheltered**, we recognize our own abilities and potential for greatness.

CAP A cap has the same significance as a hat in dreams, and draws attention to status or spiritual powers. If we are **wearing a cap** in a dream, we may be covering up our creative abilities.

CAR—*also see Journey* A car is very often representative of our personal space, an extension of our being. To dream about **being in a car** usually alerts us to our own motivation; thus, **driving a car** can indicate our need to achieve a goal, while **being a passenger** could indicate that we have handed over responsibility for our life to someone else.

CARD (GREETING) To dream about **giving or receiving a greeting card**, such as a birthday card, alerts us to the need for a specific kind of communication with the addressee. We may want to celebrate our own or others' good fortune and luck.

CARDS (PLAYING) To dream about playing cards highlights our ability to be open to opportunity or to take chances. The cards that one deals, or is dealt, in a dream may have significance.

CARRYING To be aware of **carrying an object** in a dream suggests that we need to look at what is being accepted as a burden or difficulty. If we dream about **being carried**, we may feel that we are in need of support.

CASTLE Dreaming about a castle, palace, fortress, or citadel links us to the feminine principle of the enclosed and defended private space, and can therefore be taken to represent the Great Mother. It can also represent the fantastic, or difficulty obtaining our objectives.

CATACOMB / CRYPT Many dreams contain images that have to do with space underground; to dream about a crypt or a catacomb signifies a need to come to terms with subconscious religious beliefs or training.

CATERPILLAR A caterpillar appearing in a dream usually indicates that we are undergoing some form of major change. We may be being warned that we need to undergo a complete metamorphosis—from what we are now into a greater potential.

CAULDRON The cauldron almost universally represents abundance, sustenance and nourishment. By association, the magic cauldron suggests fertility and the feminine power of transformation. To dream about a cauldron, therefore, reconnects us with our basic principles.

CAVE As with a catacomb/crypt, a cave represents a doorway into the unconscious. While initially the cave may be frightening, an exploration can reveal strong contact with our own inner selves.

CEMETERY The cemetery and its association with death can have a double meaning in dreams. It can represent the parts of ourselves that we have "killed off" or stopped using. It can also depict our thoughts and feelings about death and the attitudes and traditions surrounding it.

CENTAUR Traditionally, the Centaur was half-man and half-beast, and is associated with the Zodiac sign of Sagittarius. To have a Centaur appear in a dream demonstrates the unification of man's animal nature with his qualities of human virtue and judgment.

CENTER To dream about **being at the center** of something, such as a group of people, highlights our awareness of our ability to be powerful in a situation, or that everything revolves around us. To be **moving away** from the center indicates that part of our life may be off balance.

CEREMONY / RITUAL When we dream about taking part in a ceremony of any kind, including a religious ritual, we are conscious of a new attitude or skill that is needed, or an important change that's taking place in our life.

CHAIN To dream about chains in any form indicates a type of restriction or dependency. Just as we need strength to break out of chains, we also need strength to carry and support chains. In becoming aware of what is holding us back, we also become appreciative of how to break free.

CHALICE / CUP / GOBLET In dreams, a chalice, cup, or goblet represents the feminine, receptive principal and our ability to achieve enjoyment in different ways. We may be able to make a celebration out of something that is quite ordinary.

CHARITY To dream about **giving or receiving charity** has a lot to do with our ability to give and receive love. **A collection box** in a dream usually indicates an awareness of our own needs.

CHASED Dreaming about **being chased or trying to escape** is common; usually we are trying to escape responsibility, our own sense of failure, fear, or other emotions that we can't handle.

CHASM When we dream about a chasm or large hole, we are usually being made conscious of situations that contain some element of the unknown, or are in some way risky. We are going to have to make decisions one way or another.

CHEMIST To dream about a chemist is to link with that part of ourselves that is capable of altering the way we are. We are in touch with the wisdom—which is inherent in us all—about the Self.

CHESS—*also see Games* The game of chess originally signified the "war" between good and evil. So in dreams it may still express the conflict within. It may also indicate the need for strategy in our life.

CHEST / BOX A chest, or box, appearing in a dream delineates the way we keep hidden, or store, our emotions. Our most important ideals and hopes may need to be kept secret. It may also show the best in us—our best insights.

CHISEL The meaning of a chisel in a dream would depend on whether the dreamer is a craftsman in waking life. In such a case, it will depict pride in achievement and specialist knowledge. If the dreamer has no such skills, it will depend on other symbolism in the dream, but will probably indicate the need to use force in a situation.

CHOKE When we find ourselves choking in a dream we are coming up against our inability to express ourselves appropriately. There is some conflict between our inner and outer selves, perhaps some indecision over whether we should speak out or remain silent.

CHRYSALIS A chrysalis can be interpreted as potential for action that has not yet been realized, or as protection in a situation that requires patience.

CHURCH— *also see Religious Imagery and Temple* In dreams, a church usually represents a place of sanctuary, particularly in the sense that we can have a shared belief with other people. This may have as much to do with a shared moral code as with a code of personal behavior. A church, or church buildings, can also represent our feelings about organized religion.

CHURNING Most dreams in which there is a liquid being churned, boiled or made to move in some way links back to a very primitive sense of chaos. This indicates that we may need to reassess our creative abilities to make use of the energy available to us.

CIRCUMAMBULATION To be walking around a building or a particular spot in a dream is to be creating a "universe" in which action can take place. It is to be designating that place as having a particular significance.

CIRCUMFERENCE To be **held inside** the circumference of a circle is to be made aware through dream images of the limitations we may have placed on ourselves. To be **shut out** of the circumference of a circle is to be unworthy, or perhaps unknowing.

CITY / TOWN Dreaming about a city, particularly **one known to us**, is to be trying to understand our sense of community, of belonging to groups. We will often, through dreams, give ourselves clues as to what we require in the mental and emotional environment in which we live, and a bustling city may show our need for social interaction. **A deserted city** may portray our feelings of having been neglected by others.

CLIFF To be on **the edge of a cliff** in a dream indicates that the dreamer is facing danger. It shows the need to make a decision as to how to deal with a situation, and possibly be open to taking a risk. We are often facing the unknown.

CLIMB To dream about climbing is to dream about getting away from something, possibly to escape. We may be avoiding trouble.

CLOCK Largely, when a clock appears in a dream, we are being alerted to the passage of time. We may need to pay more attention to our own sense of timing or duty, or may need to act with a sense of urgency.

CLOSE To **be close** to someone in a dream can mean we are looking for intimacy, or perhaps protection. **To close a door** acknowledges the fact that we must make a decision to put the past behind us.

CLOTHES The clothes we wear in a dream can often depict the façade, or persona, that we create for other people. We have certain roles that we adopt in response to others' reactions. The clothes that others are wearing in our dreams can also set the scene for an acting out of some of the confrontations that take place.

CLOUDS Dreaming about clouds can have two meanings, depending on the other circumstances in the dream. It can either indicate uplifting or religious feelings, or show that we are feeling overshadowed by someone or something. It can also warn of the possibility of difficulty or danger to come.

CLUB If we dream about being in a club—a **nightclub or sports club**, for instance—we are highlighting the right of every human being to belong. If we dream about a club in the form of a weapon, it can denote an inner violence that has remained unexpressed.

COFFIN When we dream about a coffin, we are reminding ourselves of our own mortality. We may also be coming to terms with the death of a relationship and feelings of loss.

COLD To be conscious of cold in a dream is to be aware of feeling neglected, or of being left out of things.

COLORS Color is a vital part of symbolism. This has to do partly with the vibratory frequency each color has, and partly with tradition. Scientific experiments have now been carried out to ascertain what effect color has, and have proved what occultists and healers have always known—they affect our emotions and can correspond to sayings about color, such as "being green with envy" or "seeing red," to denote jealousy or anger. In working with the colors of the rainbow, we discover that warm, lively colors—which give back light—are yellow, orange and red. Cold, passive colors are blue, indigo and violet. Green is a synthesis of both warmth and cold. White light holds all color in it.

COMB A comb emphasizes the need to neaten or tidy up something in our life. We need to tidy up our thoughts.

COMET To dream about seeing a comet is to recognize the possibility of circumstances arising very quickly over which we have no control, and the outcome of which may be unavoidable.

COMPASS Dreaming about a compass is often about an attempt to find a direction or activity. We need to be able to understand the differing directions offered to us, and to follow the one that is right for us.

COMPUTER The computer is now such a part of people's lives that it very much depends on other circumstances in the dream as to the correct interpretation of this image. If one **works with computers**, it may simply be a means to an end, whereas in other cases it will be a reminder of personal potential or abilities.

COOKING To be cooking in a dream is to be preparing nourishment or to be satisfying a hunger, whether our own or other people's. This hunger may not be as straightforward as a physical hunger, but something more subtle, such as a need to make use of the varied opportunities available to us.

CORNER To turn a corner in a dream indicates that we have succeeded in moving forward into new experiences, despite what may have seemed to be obstacles in front of us. Turning **right at a corner** indicates a logical course of action, whereas **turning left** indicates a more intuitive approach.

COUNTRYSIDE—*also see Places* When we dream about the countryside we are putting ourselves in touch with our own natural, spontaneous feelings. We may have memories of the countryside that invoke a particular mood, state, or way of being. We can return, without feeling guilty, to a very relaxed state.

CRAB A crab appearing in a dream can indicate mothering, particularly of the smothering type, but can also be the qualities of unreliability and self-interest. The crab can also, because of the way it moves, denote deviousness.

CRADLE To dream about a cradle can represent new life or new beginnings. As a **precognitive dream**, a cradle can represent a forthcoming pregnancy, or, if this is highly unlikely, it can also represent the need to return to a womblike, protected state.

CRACK Dreaming about something that is cracked indicates our recognition of something that is flawed in our life. There may be a weakness or difficulty in the attitudes and defenses that we use to meet life's problems.

CRANE When we dream about a **building crane** we are often being told of the need to raise our level of awareness in some matter. We need to make an attempt to understand the overall or universal implications of our actions.

CROCODILE To dream of crocodiles, or any reptile, indicates that we are looking at the frightening lower aspects of our nature. We may feel we have no control over these, and it would therefore be very easy to be devoured by them.

CROOKED LINE When any kind of line appears in a dream as crooked, there is usually a need to register something as being out of balance or off-kilter, or there may be some insincerity in our dealings with others.

CROSSING To dream of **crossing a road** is recognizing the possibility of danger, fear, or uncertainty. We are perhaps pitting ourselves against the majority, or something that is bigger than us.

CROSSROADS / INTERSECTION Dreaming of crossroads, or an intersection, indicates that we are going to have to make choices in our life. Often, to **turn left** at a crossroads can indicate taking the wrong route, although it can also indicate the more intuitive path. To **turn right** therefore tends to mean taking the correct path, or making a logical decision.

CROWD Dreaming about being in a crowd could indicate that we don't wish to stand out, or that we don't have a sense of direction at present. We may wish to camouflage our feelings from others, to get lost, or even to hide our opinions.

CROWN To dream of a crown is to acknowledge one's own success and to recognize that we have opportunities that will expand our knowledge and awareness. We may be about to receive an honor or reward of some kind.

CRUTCH When we dream of crutches, we are experiencing the need for support, although it might also be that we need to support others. We may find others inadequate, and need to readjust our thinking.

D: Dagger to Drunk

DAGGER When a dagger appears in a dream, the meaning can be either aggressive or defensive. If the dreamer is **using the dagger** to attack someone, then he or she may be trying to cut out some part of themselves or to get rid of something they do not like. If the dreamer is **being stabbed**, they are highlighting their vulnerability.

DAM—*also see Water* When we dream about a dam, we might be bottling up our own emotions and drive or, conversely, we could be trying to stop somebody else's emotional outburst from happening. To be **building a dam** indicates that we are likely to be putting up defenses, whereas if a **dam is bursting** we might feel we have no control over emotional situations around us.

DANCING Dance has always represented freedom and been symbolic of other actions that were necessary for survival. To be dancing in a dream portrays the creation of happiness, feeling at one with the surroundings and possibly getting closer or more intimate with a partner.

DANGER When we find ourselves in dangerous circumstances in dreams, we are often reflecting the anxieties and dilemmas of everyday life. We might be conscious that our activities could be harmful to us if we carry on in the same way.

DARK To dream about **being in the dark** usually represents a state of confusion or being in unknown and difficult territory. It may point to a secret part of ourselves or a part we do not yet know.

DATE When a calendar date is highlighted in a dream, we are either being reminded of something particularly significant—or possibly traumatic—in our life, or being asked to consider the potential symbolism of the numbers contained in the date itself. Meanwhile, when we dream about the fruit known as a date, we are becoming conscious of the need for the rare or exotic in our life. Equally, we may need sweetness and nurturing.

DAWN To dream about a dawn or a new day represents a new beginning or a new awareness in circumstances around us. We are looking for different ways of dealing with old situations.

DAY When we dream about a day passing, or register that time has passed, we are alerting ourselves to the fact that we need to gauge time in some activity, or that action needs to be taken first before a second thing can happen.

DEAD END When the dreamer finds that he or she is **trapped in a dead end**, it symbolizes a futile action, but perhaps also a state of inertia. Circumstances might be preventing forward movement, and it might be necessary to retrace one's steps in order to succeed.

DEAD PEOPLE Dead people we have known appearing in dreams usually refer to strong emotions we have had about those people, whether they are negative or positive. For instance, we might hold unresolved anger or guilt, and the only way we can deal with it is in a dream sequence. It can also be a comforting experience to see a dead loved one who has recently passed away.

DEATH Traditionally, to dream about death indicated the possibility of a birth or a change in circumstances in one's own life or that of people around us. Because in the past death held great fear, it also represented calamity, in the sense that nothing would ever be the same again. It was something that had to be experienced and endured rather than understood. As people's attitudes have changed, death in a dream has come to indicate a challenge that we must confront—a need to adjust our approach to life, and to accept that there can be a new beginning if we have the courage to go for it. To **dream about our own death** means that we are exploring our own feelings about death—the retreat from the challenge of life or the split between mind and body.

DEEP When we dream about the deep, we are usually considering past family influences of which we may not be consciously mindful.

DEMOLITION It depends on the circumstances in the dream whether demolition highlights major changes in the dreamer's life, or a self-inflicted trauma. If we are **carrying out the demolition**, we need to be in control; but if **someone else** is in charge, we might feel powerless in the face of change.

DEPARTING—*also see Journey* To be departing from a known situation such as **leaving home** indicates a breaking away from old or habitual patterns of behavior. We may need to give ourselves the freedom to be independent.

DESCENT / DESCENDING When we dream about a descent, such as **coming down a mountain or steps**, we are often searching for an answer to a particular problem and need to be conscious of past trauma or something that we have left behind and what we can learn from it.

DESERT To dream about **being alone in a desert** signifies a lack of emotional satisfaction, loneliness, or perhaps isolation. Dreaming about **being in a desert with someone** else may show us that the relationship is sterile, or is going nowhere.

DESK—*also see Table* If the desk we are dreaming about is an old one, such as our old **school desk, or an antique**, perhaps we should be returning to old values, habits, or disciplines. If it is a **work or office desk**, we may need to consider the way in which we are carrying out our everyday life.

DESTINATION—*also see Places* It is fairly common to dream about trying to get to a particular destination, and it normally indicates a conscious ambition and desire. If the **destination is not known to us**, we may be moving into unknown territory, or be attempting something new and different.

DEVIL To dream about a devil or fiend usually means that we have to come to terms with a part of ourselves that is frightening and/or unknown. We need to confront this part and make it work for us rather than against us. And to dream about the conventional figure of the Devil, with horns and a tail, means that something difficult needs to be confronted in order for it to lose its potency.

DEW Dew or gentle rain falling in a dream can represent a sense of newness and refreshment that we have perhaps not been able to obtain, except from an external source.

DICE / DIE To be **playing with dice** in a dream emphasizes the fact that we are playing with fate or taking chances in life that we really ought to be considering more carefully.

DIGGING / EXCAVATION—*also see Mines* Often, when we begin the process of learning about ourselves, we need to uncover parts that we have kept hidden, and this is shown in dreams as excavating a hole or digging up an object.

DINOSAUR When we dream about monsters or prehistoric animals we are touching on basic images that have the power to both frighten and amaze us—and even to threaten our existence. Because they are considered to be so large, we need to be aware of whether it is their size or their power that is frightening.

DIRTY We tend to dream about **being dirty** when we are not operating within our own principles, or when someone else's action has put us in a situation in which we find ourselves compromised.

DIVING To dream about diving can represent the need for freedom in our life, although we may associate freedom with taking risks. We may need to burrow into our unconscious to find the ability to face anxiety. Taking such risks is a vital part of enabling us to have a more expansive experience of life.

DIVORCE Dreaming about divorce can signify our need to be free of responsibilities or of separation from a particular person in the dream. It may also indicate the necessity to clarify our relationship between the various facets of our personality.

DOCTOR When we dream about a doctor, we are aware that we need to give way to a higher authority in health matters.

DOG—*also see Animals* Dreaming about a dog depends on whether it is one known to us (such as a childhood pet)—when it may represent happy memories—or whether it is **unknown** to us, which may signify the qualities of loyalty and unconditional love associated with dogs.

DOLL A doll can depict either how the dreamer felt as a child, or a need for comfort. It may also express an undeveloped part of the dreamer's personality.

DOLPHIN—*also see Animals* Dolphins are perceived as saviors and guides that have special knowledge and awareness. Coming from the depths—the unconscious—they also represent the hidden sides of ourselves that need to be understood.

DRAFT To **feel a draft** in a dream is to be aware of an external force that could affect us or a particular situation that we are in. To **create a draft** is to be attempting to clear the atmosphere.

DRAGON The dragon is a complex symbol. Seen as frightening yet manageable, under certain circumstances it will represent in us our own untamed nature—our own passions and chaotic beliefs with which we must come to terms. Often we can only achieve this through dreams, in an environment that has been suitably created.

DRINK To be drinking in a dream is to be absorbing or taking something in. **What we are drinking** is also important, e.g. fruit juice would indicate that we are aware of the need for cleansing and purity.

DROWNING—*also see Swimming* When we are drowning in a dream, it usually indicates that we are fearful of allowing our emotions free expression and/or in danger of being overwhelmed by emotions that we cannot handle. Drowning might also indicate an inability to handle a stressful situation.

DRUGS—*also see Intoxication* When drugs appear in a dream, whether self-administered or not, it suggests that we may need external help to enable us to change our inner perceptions. **To be taking drugs** suggests that we feel we have relinquished control of a situation in our waking life and are having to rely on external stimuli. **To have an adverse drug reaction** could mean that we fear madness. **To be given drugs against our will** indicates that we may be being forced to accept an unpalatable truth.

DRUM—*also see Musical Instruments* To **hear a drum** in a dream indicates that we need to be more in touch with our natural rhythms and primitive urges to stay sane and healthy. To be **playing a drum** is to be taking responsibility for the rhythm of our own life.

DRUNK—*also see Alcohol and Intoxication* **To be drunk** in a dream means that we are abandoning ourselves to irrational forces. We want to be free of responsibility and free of inhibitions. **To make someone else drunk** is to be forcing our irresponsibility onto someone else.

E: Eagle to Explosion

EAGLE—*also see Birds* An eagle appearing in a dream signifies inspiration and strength. It may also indicate our need to ascend, in order to release ourselves from old ideas or attitudes. As a bird of prey, the eagle is capable of making use of all the opportunities available to it. Dreaming about one shows that we can do likewise.

EARTH To dream about the **planet Earth** is to take account of the supportive network that we have in place in our life, and the attitudes and relationships we take for granted. We are searching for some kind of parental love or social order. **Soil or soft earth** particularly links with the need for mothering or tactile contact.

EARTHQUAKE Dreaming about an earthquake alerts us to an inner insecurity that we must deal with before it overwhelms us. There is great inner change and growth taking place that could cause upheaval.

EATING—*also see Food and Nourishment* **To be eating** in a dream shows that one is attempting to satisfy one's needs or hunger. Hunger is a basic drive, and we need to realize that only once such a drive is met can we move forward to satisfying our more aesthetic needs. When we dream about **being eaten** we are facing our fear of losing our sense of identity, of being consumed by something such as an obsession, an overwhelming emotion or drive, or of having to deal with something we cannot control.

ECLIPSE—*also see Moon and Planets* Dreaming about an eclipse signifies our fears and doubts about our own success. Others around us seem to be more important or able than we are, which does not allow us to excel at what we are doing.

EDUCATION—*also see School and Teacher* To dream about a place of education, such as **a school, college or university**, indicates that we should be considering our own need for discipline or disciplined action. We are perhaps inadequately prepared for a task we are to perform, and need to access more knowledge.

EGG The egg is the symbol of unrealized potential, of possibilities yet to come. Because of this, to dream about an egg indicates that we have not made fully conscious our natural abilities. To be **eating an egg** shows the need to take in certain aspects of newness before we can fully explore a different way of life.

ELECTRICITY Electricity often represents power, and it will depend on the context of the dream which aspect of power is being highlighted. To dream about electrical **wires** is to be aware of the dreamer's capability, whereas to dream about **switches** is to be aware of the ability to control.

ELOPING Dreaming about eloping, particularly **with someone you know**, is trying to escape from a situation that could ultimately be painful. We must maintain a balance between the need for emotional and material security.

EMBRYO To dream about an embryo or fetus is to become aware of an extremely vulnerable part of ourselves. We may also be making ourselves aware of a situation in our life that is just beginning—one that has not moved beyond a germ of an idea.

EMOTIONS In the context of a dream, our emotions can be very different from those we have in everyday life. They might be more extreme, for instance, as though we have at last given ourselves full freedom of expression.

EMPLOYMENT Dreams about employment often have to do with what we consider our "calling" to be, rather than what we actually do. Since employment can also represent the way other people think and feel about us, such a dream will tend to be about us assessing our own worth.

EMPTINESS To experience emptiness in a dream indicates that there might be a lack of pleasure, purpose, direction, and enthusiasm in our life. We could be suffering from a sense of isolation, or perhaps of not having anything to hold onto.

ENCLOSED / ENCLOSURE In dreams, the defense mechanisms we put in place to prevent ourselves from deeply feeling the impact of such things as relationships, love, anxiety, or pain can often manifest as an enclosed space. Restraints and constraints can appear as actual walls and barriers.

END To dream about there being an ending to something signifies the reaching of a goal or a point at which things must inevitably change. We need to decide what we value most, and therefore what we can leave behind and what must be taken forward.

ENGINE—*also see Car* The motivating drive or energy we need in a situation can be perceived in dreams as an engine. When the dream seems to concentrate on the mechanical action of the engine, we might need to look at the more dynamic, pragmatic ways of dealing with our life. To be **removing the engine** could indicate a serious health problem.

ENGINEERING To dream about engineering is to connect with our ability to construct something that will allow us either to move forward or to make life easier for ourselves. To dream about engineering works—as in **roadwork**—is to recognize the need for some adjustment in part of our life.

ENTRANCE—*also see Door* An entrance in a dream represents a new experience, or area of experience, often signifying the need to make changes, to create new opportunities, or perhaps to explore the unknown.

ESCAPE When we dream about escape, we are trying to move beyond—or avoid—difficult feelings. We might be trying to run away from a duty.

EVAPORATION To be aware of water in a dream and then realize that it has evaporated is to recognize the transformation that can take place once emotion is dealt with correctly.

EVERGREENS Dreaming about evergreen trees can represent the need for vitality and freshness, for youth and vigor, and sometimes for cleansing.

EVENING When we are aware of it being evening in a dream, we need to recognize the fact that we need time for ourselves—perhaps relaxation and quiet peace.

EVIL To experience evil in a dream is usually to be conscious of our own urges, which we have judged to be wrong. Other aspects of evil, such as inappropriate action by others, may be experienced as dread and disgust.

EXAMS / BEING EXAMINED Dreaming about examinations or tests (particularly educational ones) is usually connected with self-assessment, self-criticism and the need for high achievement. We might be allowing others to set our standards of morality and success for us. **Being examined by a doctor** might alert us to the need to watch our health. **A driving test** might suggest a test of confidence or ability, whereas a **written test** is likely to signify a test of knowledge.

EXPLOSION An explosion in a dream usually indicates a release of energy in a forceful way that will allow us to make changes in the way we express ourselves. Usually the emotion behind the explosion will be considered a negative one that we may have suppressed for some time.

F: Fabulous Beasts to Future

FABULOUS BEASTS *such as Griffins, Unicorns or Minotaurs* In dream imagery, in order to draw the dreamer's attention to certain qualities, animals might be shown as having characteristics belonging to other creatures. The dreamer is being shown through this that there is freedom from convention.

FACE To concentrate on **somebody else's face** in a dream is an attempt to understand the outward personality. To be **looking at our own face** means that we might be trying to come to terms with the way we express ourselves in the ordinary, everyday world. When the **face is hidden**, we are hiding our own power, or refusing to acknowledge our own abilities.

FAILURE Failure in a dream may not necessarily be personal. If, for instance, **lights fail or refuse to work**, we might need to be aware of a lack of energy or power. **Personal failure** can indicate a degree of competitiveness, or offer alternatives in the way we need to act.

FAIRY Because fairies are representations of elemental forces, for them to appear in a dream signifies our connection with those forces in ourselves. It could be that the lighter side of our nature is being highlighted, or it might be the more malign side, as in goblins and elves.

FAIRGROUND To dream about **being in a fairground** might represent a reconnection to the lighthearted, childlike side of ourselves. We can afford to be less inhibited in public. To be attending **a carnival or fiesta** means we can drop whatever constraints or restraints we may impose on ourselves or others.

FALL / FALLING If we dream about the season Fall, we are being made conscious of the sense of something coming to an end. We realize that the good in a situation can be recognized, and made use of, but the rest must be given up. **A fall**, in the other sense, outlines the need to be grounded—to take care in a known situation. And to dream about **falling** shows a lack of confidence in our own ability. We might feel threatened by a lack of security, whether real or imagined. Or we might fear being dropped by friends or colleagues.

FAME Dreaming about **being famous** or **achieving fame in a chosen field** signifies that we ourselves need to recognize and give ourselves credit for our own abilities. In waking life we may be relatively shy, but in dreams we can often achieve things of which we would not believe we were capable.

FAMILY The family is the first basic security image a child has. Often, through circumstances that are not in that child's control, that image becomes distorted, and dreams will either attempt to put this image right or will confirm the distortion. Thus, we might dream about an **argument with a family member**, but the interpretation will depend on both the circumstances of the dream and our everyday relationship with that person.

FAMOUS PEOPLE / MOVIE STARS In dreams a movie star, pop star or public figure will represent their ideal. A young person dreaming about a movie star might not be ready for the responsibility of a real relationship.

FAN Dreaming about a fan connects with the feminine side of one's nature and the intuitive forces. Particularly **in a woman's dream**, a fan can represent sensuality and sexuality.

FARE To be **paying a fare** in a dream is acknowledging the price that is paid in order to succeed. A **taxi fare** would imply a more private process than a **bus fare**.

FARM / FARMYARD—*also see Animals* To be in a farmyard in a dream (if it is not a memory) shows us as being in touch with the down-to-earth side of ourselves. There are many facets of behavior that can be interpreted in animal terms—for example, to be "as gentle as a lamb"—and often this type of dream has more impact than one that includes people.

FASTING To be fasting in a dream may be an attempt to come to terms with some emotional trauma, or to draw attention to the need for cleansing in some way.

FAT To dream about being fat alerts the dreamer to the defenses used against inadequacy. Equally, we might be conscious of the sensual and fun side of ourselves that we have not been expressing.

FATIGUE **Feeling fatigue** in a dream might indicate that we should be looking at health matters, or that we are not using our energies in an appropriate way.

FEATHER Feathers in a dream could denote softness and lightness, perhaps a more gentle approach to a situation. We might need to look at the truth in the particular situation and recognize that we need to be calmer and more collected in what we are doing.

FENCE When we dream about fences, we are dreaming about social or class barriers, or perhaps our own need for privacy. We might be aware of boundaries in relationships that can prevent us from achieving the type of connection we need. We might have difficulty expressing ourselves in some way.

FERMENTATION To dream about the process of fermentation indicates that events are occurring in the background that we must wait for to develop.

FERRY To dream about **being on a ferry** indicates that we are making some movement toward change. Because a ferry carries large numbers of people, it might also represent a group to which we belong needing to change its way of working and take responsibility for moving as a group rather than as individuals.

FIELD When we dream we're in a field, we are looking at our field of activity—what we are doing in everyday life. It might also be a play on words relating to how we "feel."

FIG OR FIG TREE Often, because of its shape, the fig is associated with sexuality, fertility, masculinity, and prosperity. To dream about **eating figs** might be a recognition that some kind of celebration is necessary, or that a situation holds more potential than we thought at first.

FIGHT If we dream that we are **in a fight**, it usually indicates that we are confronting our need for independence. It can also mean that we need to express underlying anger and frustration, and/or that we have a subconscious desire to hurt either a part of ourselves or someone else—something that would be unacceptable in the waking state.

FILES / FILING To dream about files or filing is about putting order into our life—making sense of what we are doing and how we are doing it. To be **filing things away** might indicate that we no longer need to be aware of a particular situation, but that we still need to retain the knowledge an experience has given us.

FIND If we dream about finding something, such as a precious object, we are becoming aware of a part of ourselves that is, or will be, of use to us. We are making a discovery or a realization that, depending on the rest of the dream scenario, may be about us or about others.

FIRE Fire in a dream can suggest passion and desire in its more positive sense, and frustration, anger, resentment, and destructiveness in its more negative. It will depend on whether the fire is **controlled** or otherwise on the exact interpretation. To be more conscious of the **flame** of the fire would be to be aware of the energy and strength that is being created. Being aware of the **heat** of a fire is to be aware of someone else's strong feelings. To be **lighting or tending** a fire indicates a need for cleansing some aspect of our life.

FIRE BUCKET As a symbol, a fire bucket indicates that we may have a situation around us that is out of control. It is only by a display of "dampening" emotion that there can be any progress. Someone might have gone to an extreme, and need help.

FIREWORKS Fireworks are generally accepted as belonging to a happy occasion or celebration, though they may also be frightening. When we dream about fireworks, we are hoping to be able to celebrate good fortune, although there might be a secondary emotion associated with that celebration.

FISH Dreaming about fish connects with the emotional side of ourselves, but more our ability to be wise without being strategic. We can often simply respond instinctively to what is going on, without needing to analyze it.

FISHERMAN A fisherman in a dream will often represent a provider, or perhaps bravery, as with a **deep-sea fisherman**, whereas a **freshwater fisherman** may indicate the need for rest and recuperation.

FLAG A flag in a dream will have the same meaning as a banner—that is, a standard or a place around which people with common aims and beliefs can gather. It may represent old-fashioned principles and beliefs.

FLEAS Fleas are an irritation, and in dreams signify just that—a symbol that there might be people or situations in our life that are causing us difficulty, or that we feel are being parasites, and that we need to go through a process of decontamination in order to be free of.

FLIES To dream about flies is to be aware that we have certain negative aspects of our life that need to be dealt with. To dream about **a swarm of flies** is to dream about the type of purposeful behavior that occurs when there are large numbers of insects. Although one insect appears to be moving aimlessly, large numbers do not. Often we can only succeed in changing matters via group behavior or a collective dynamic.

FLIGHT / FLYING—*also see Journey* Conventionally, to dream about flying has to do with sex and sexuality, but it would probably be more accurate to look at it in terms of lack of inhibition and freedom. We are releasing ourselves from limitations that we may impose on ourselves.

FLOATING Floating in a dream was considered by Freud to be connected with sexuality, but it is likely that it has much more to do with the inherent need for freedom. Generally, we are opening to a power beyond our conscious self, being carried along apparently beyond our own volition. We are in a state of extreme relaxation and are simply allowing events to carry us along.

FLOCK To dream about a flock—for instance of **birds or sheep**—is to recognize the need to belong to a group, to have a common aim or way of being.

FLOGGING To dream about **being flogged** can indicate that we are aware that someone is driving us beyond our limits, often in an inappropriate manner. **Flogging ourselves** would highlight a type of masochism in us.

FLOOD—*also see Water* Flood dreams are fascinating, because while they are frightening, they often indicate a release of positive energy. Usually it is an overflow of repressed or unconscious feelings that needs to be moved out of the way before progress can be made. To be **in the middle of a flood** indicates that we might be feeling overwhelmed by these feelings, whereas **watching a flood** suggests that we are simply watching ourselves. Often a flood dream can indicate depression.

FLOWERS Flowers in a dream usually give us the opportunity to link to feelings of pleasure and beauty. We are aware that something new, perhaps a feeling or ability, is beginning to come into being, and that there is a freshness about what we are doing. **To be given a bouquet** means that we are being rewarded for an action—the color of the flowers might be important *(see Colors)*. In folklore, each type of flower had a meaning in dreams:

Anemone Untrustworthiness in someone we know.

Arum Lily An unhappy marriage or the death of a relationship.

Bluebell Argumentativeness.

Buttercup An increase in business.

Carnation A passionate love affair.

Clover Good fortune, or someone in need of finance may try to get in touch.

Crocus Darkness and lack of trust.

Daffodil Unfairness and reconciliation.

Daisy Innocence and purity.

Forget-me-not A partner in your life may not be able to give you what you need.

Geranium A recent quarrel is not as serious as you thought.

Honeysuckle You will be upset by domestic quarrels.

Iris Good news to come.

Lime/Linden Feminine grace.

Marigold Possible business difficulties.

Mistletoe A time of celebration, love, partnership, and the need for constancy.

Myrtle Peace, tranquility, happiness, joy, and constancy.

Narcissus Don't mistake shadow for substance.

Peony Excessive self-restraint may cause you distress.

Poppy A symbol of sacrifice (as in the Veterans Day and Memorial Day poppy)—or of idleness and oblivion (as in the opium poppy).

Primrose You will find happiness in a new friendship.

Rose Love, and perhaps a wedding soon.

Snowdrop The need to confide in someone rather than hide problems.

Violet Marriage to someone younger.

FLUTE—*also see Musical Instruments* Many musical instruments, particularly wind instruments, indicate extremes of emotion, enticement and flattery. The flute is sometimes said to stand for anguish.

FOG To dream about being in fog indicates our confusion and inability to confront, or often even to see, the real issues at stake in our life. We are often confused by external matters and the impact they might have on us emotionally.

FOLLOW If we are **following someone** or something in a dream, we might need a cause or crusade to help give us a sense of identity. We are looking for leadership or are aware how much we can be influenced by other people. It also indicates that, particularly in a work situation, we might be more comfortable in a secondary position rather than out in front.

FOOD—*also see Eating and Nourishment* Food signifies a satisfaction of our basic needs, whether physical, mental, or spiritual. Frequent dreams about eating or drinking suggest a great hunger or thirst for an outcome.

FOOTPRINTS To see footprints in a dream indicates that we need to follow someone or their way of being. If the footprints are **in front of us**, there is help available to us in the future; but if they are **behind us**, perhaps we need to look at the way we have done things in the past. They usually indicate help in one way or another.

FOREST—*also see Trees and Wood* Dreaming about forests or a group of trees usually means entering the realms of the feminine. A forest is often a place of testing and initiation. It always has to do with coming to terms with our emotional self, of understanding the secrets of our own nature, or of our own spiritual world.

FORK A fork, particularly a three-pronged one, is often considered the symbol of the Devil, and therefore can symbolize evil and trickery. In dreams, a fork denotes duality and indecision.

FORGE When the forge and the blacksmith were a part of normal, everyday life, this dream would indicate some aspect of hard work or desire to reach a goal. Now it is more likely to mean a ritual action.

FOUNTAIN To dream about a fountain means we're aware of the process of life and the "flow" of our own consciousness. Because of its connection with water *(see Water)*, it also represents the surge of our emotions, and often our ability to express this. The fountain can also represent an element of play in our life.

FRAUD When fraud appears in a dream, particularly if the dreamer is **being defrauded**, there is the potential to be too trusting of people. If the dreamer is the one **committing fraud**, he or she runs the risk of losing a good friend.

FRIEND Friends appearing in our dreams can signify one of two things. Either we need to look at our relationship with that person, or we need to decide what that friend represents to us (for instance security, support and love).

FROG—*also see Animals* Many people associate the frog with a visible growth pattern that mirrors the growth to maturity of a human being. In dreams, to see a frog at a particular stage of its growth depicts the feeling we have about ourselves. For instance, to see it at the stage where it has grown back legs would suggest that we are capable of moving forward by leaps and bounds.

FRUIT—*also see Food* To dream about fruit, particularly in a bowl, very often indicates the culmination of actions we have taken in the past. We have been able to "harvest" the past and make a new beginning for ourselves.

FUNERAL—*also see Mourning* To dream about **being at a funeral** indicates that we need to come to terms with our feelings about death. This might not necessarily be our own death, but the death of others. It might also indicate a period of mourning for something that has happened in the past, and this period can allow us to move forward into the future. To dream about our **own funeral** can indicate a desire for sympathy. It might also indicate that a part of us is dead and we have to let it go.

FURNITURE / FURNISHINGS The furniture that appears in our dreams, particularly if it is drawn to our attention, often shows how we feel about our family and home life, and what attitudes or habits we have developed. It can also give an indication as to how we feel about ourselves. For instance, **dark, heavy material** might suggest the possibility of depression.

FUTURE If in a dream we are aware that events will take place in the future of our dream, they usually have to do with actions that we need to take in waking life. We also might have precognitive dreams, which is when we dream about events before they take place in waking life, and recognize that we already "knew" about them. The theory behind this is that the past, present, and future coexist, and that it is possible to "read" these records in the dream state. Our experience of them is subjective, although we are in the position of observers.

G: Games to Guru

GAMES / GAMBLING Playing a game in our dream indicates that we are taking note of how we play the game of life. If we are **playing well**, we may take it that we are coping well with circumstances in our life. If we are **playing badly**, we might need to reassess our abilities and identify which skills we need to improve in order to do things better. Games and gambling can also represent not taking life seriously. They can show how we work in the competitive field, and give us insight into our own sense of winning or losing.

GARBAGE Garbage in our dreams creates a scenario where we are able to deal with those parts of our experience or our feelings that are like garbage, and need to be examined in order to decide what is to be kept and what is to be rejected. To be **collecting garbage** can indicate that we are making wrong assumptions.

GARDEN Dreaming about a garden can be fascinating, because it might indicate an area of growth in our own life; it could also be something we're trying to cultivate in ourselves.

GARDENER Often a gardener indicates someone wise on whom we can rely, who will take care of those things with which we do not feel capable of dealing.

GARLAND Depending on the type of garland in the dream, we are recognizing some distinction or honor for ourselves. If we are **wearing a garland**, such as a **Hawaiian lei**, we are looking at ways of making ourselves happy. We are looking at dedication, and at some way of setting ourselves apart from others.

GARLIC Garlic is often either a symbol of fertility (due to its form) or of protection (due to its strong smell).

GASOLINE Gasoline is a form of energy, and in dreams it is recognized as something we need in order to keep ourselves going. For instance, to **put gasoline into a vehicle** might indicate that we need to take better care of our body. Gasoline is also explosive and dangerous, so to **use gasoline in a dangerous way** could mean we're making problems for ourselves in some situation in our everyday life.

GATE Dreaming about a gate usually signifies some kind of change, often in awareness. We are passing a threshold in our life, perhaps trying something different or moving from one phase of life to another.

GHOST Dreaming of a ghost links us to old habit patterns or buried hopes and longings. There is something insubstantial in these, possibly because we have not put enough energy into them.

GIANT Dreaming about giants might mean we are coming to terms with some of the repressed feelings we had about adults when we were children. They may have seemed larger than life or frightening in some way.

GIVING To dream about giving somebody something in a dream indicates our need to give and take in a relationship—our need to give of ourselves, perhaps to share with others what we have, and to create an environment that allows for give and take.

GLASS Dreaming about glass indicates the invisible but very tangible barriers we might erect around ourselves in order to protect ourselves from relationships with other people. It could also represent the barriers other people put up, and or the aspects of ourselves we have built up in our own defense.

GLASSES For glasses to stand out in a dream indicates a connection with our ability to see or to understand. Equally, if **someone is unexpectedly wearing glasses**, it has to do either with our lack of understanding, or with their inability to see where we are coming from.

GLOBE To dream about looking at a globe, or the world beyond our sphere, suggests the need for a wider viewpoint on a particular situation.

GLOOM If there is a sense of gloom in a dream, it can indicate difficulty seeing or comprehending things from an external viewpoint. There could be negativity of which we have to be aware in order to dispel it—to create light and clarity—so we can continue with our life.

GLOVES Because gloves used to be a big part of social etiquette, they represented honor and purity. Today, being aware of gloves in a dream often represents some way in which we are hiding our abilities from people around us. To **take off gloves** signifies respect and an act of sincerity. To dream about **boxing gloves** could indicate that we are trying too hard to succeed in a situation where there is aggression.

GOAL To dream about **scoring a goal** might indicate that we have set ourselves external targets. In achieving those targets, we might also recognize that we need to adjust the goals we have set for ourselves. **To miss a goal** indicates that we haven't taken all the circumstances of a situation into account, and perhaps we need to reassess our ability to achieve.

GOD / GODS When we dream about God, we are acknowledging to ourselves that there is a higher power in charge. We connect with all of humanity, and therefore have a right to a set of moral beliefs.

GODDESS / GODDESSES Dreaming about **mythical goddesses** connects us with our archetypal images of femininity. **In a woman's dream**, a goddess will clarify the connection through the unconscious that exists between all women and female creatures. It is a sense of mystery, of a shared secret, that is such an intangible force in the woman's psyche. In the waking state it is that which enables women to create a sisterhood or network among themselves in order to bring about a common aim. **In a man's dream**, the goddess figure signifies all that a man fears in the concept of female power. It usually also gives an insight into his earliest view of femininity through his experience of his mother.

GOGGLES—*also see Glasses and Mask* Goggles can be used to cover the eyes (often believed to be the seat of the soul), or to enable us to see better. Under most circumstances, dreaming about them is a sign of the latter (looking and seeing more clearly), but sometimes they indicate that we need more protection in waking life.

GOLD Gold in dreams suggests the best, most valuable aspects of ourselves. **Finding gold** indicates that we can discover those characteristics in ourselves or others. **Burying gold** shows that we are trying to hide something—perhaps information or knowledge.

GONG To **hear the sound of a gong** in a dream is to be aware that some limitation has been reached, or conversely that permission has been given for further action. **To strike the gong** may represent the need for strength and the need to achieve a quality of sound or information in a waking situation.

GOSSIP **To be gossiping** in a dream can mean that one is spreading information, but in a way that is not necessarily appropriate. To be in a group of people and **listening to gossip** generally means that we are looking for some kind of information, but perhaps do not have the ability to achieve it for ourselves. We have to use other people to enable us to achieve the correct level of information.

GRAIL The Holy Grail is such a basic image that in dreams it can appear as something miraculous, something that fulfills our wish and allows us to move forward into our full potential. Often it represents the achievement of spiritual success, but it can also represent the cup of happiness. The grail appearing in a dream would indicate that we can expect some form of satisfaction and change to occur in our life.

GRAIN Dreaming about grains such as wheat, oats, barley, etc., can indicate a kind of harvest, where opportunities we have created for ourselves can come to fruition. As long as we pay attention to the outcome of these opportunities, we can take that success forward and create even more abundance.

GRAMMAR When we become conscious of grammar in dreams, we are aware of our own or others' difficulty in communicating.

GRAPES—*also see Fruit*

To see grapes in a dream generally indicates that there is a need for celebration. The grape is the fruit most closely associated with Bacchus or, in his Greek form, Dionysus, the god of conviviality. To dream about grapes indicates the search for fun, laughter and creativity in our life.

GRASS Grass is often a symbol of new growth, and of victory over barrenness.

GRASSHOPPER The grasshopper is a symbol of freedom and capriciousness, and in dreams it can often indicate a bid for freedom.

GRAVE—*also see Death* Dreaming about a grave is an indication that we must have regard for our feelings about, or our concept of, death. Such a dream may also be attempting to deal with our feelings about someone who has died.

GRAVEL Often our attention is drawn to the size of items in a dream. Gravel in this context is simply an indication of small particles. Such a dream might also bring back memories of a time or place, and remind us of happier times.

GREASE Grease in a dream makes us aware that perhaps we have not been as careful in a situation as we should have been. We have created circumstances that do not give us an advantage, and could be "slippery" or uncomfortable.

GROWTH The changes in us that bring about new ways of relating to other people, who we are, or situations around us, are all stages of growth. They can be pictured in dreams as the growth of a plant or something similar.

GUILLOTINE A guillotine in a dream indicates something irrational in our personality. We might be afraid of losing self-control, or of having part of our personality amputated. We could be aware of an injury to our person or to our dignity.

GUITAR Guitar music in a dream can foretell the possibility of a new romance, but can also indicate the need for caution. **If the dreamer is playing the guitar**, he or she is making an attempt to be more creative.

GUN—*also see Weapons* In dreams, a gun has an obvious masculine and sexual connotation. **If a woman is firing** a gun, she is aware of the masculine, aggressive side of her personality. **If she is being shot at**, she perhaps feels threatened by overt signs of aggression or sexuality.

H: Hail to Huntsman

HAIL Because it is frozen water *(see Ice)*, hail in a dream signifies the freezing of our emotions. It would appear that the danger and damage created by these frozen emotions comes from outside influences rather than internal feelings.

HAIRSTYLIST In dreams, a hairstylist may appear as the part of ourselves that deals with self-image and the way we feel about ourselves. We perhaps need to consider ways in which we can change our image.

HALF Dreams can often have a peculiar quality in that our image may only be half there or we perhaps only experience half an action. This usually indicates an incompleteness in us, a sort of in-between state that means that we have to make decisions. Often it is about going forward into the future or back into the past: completion or non-completion. For instance, we might have half-completed a task, and be aware of this, but do not know how to finish it. Often the dream images that appear can show us how to do this. Conversely, if in a dream we have only **partially completed a task** and are left feeling dissatisfied with what has happened, we might need to consider in waking life what needs to be done to enable us to complete the action in the dream. What would we have done had we been able to complete it?

HALLUCINATIONS There is a hallucinatory quality to dreams. Scenes can change or merge into one another in the blink of an eye; objects can take on the qualities of people; and we are likely to see and do things that in waking life would seem completely surreal. But it's all totally acceptable in a dream. It is only when we consider the dream on waking that we realize how odd it all was. Freed from the logical quality that mentors our everyday life, we can be liberated to create a new awareness of our own abilities, thought patterns, and even our past.

HAMMER Dreaming about hammers or other blunt instruments highlights the more aggressive and masculine side of our nature, and indicates that we may be using undue force or power to achieve a certain outcome.

HANDCUFFS Dreaming about **being in handcuffs** denotes that we have been restrained in some way, often by an authority figure.

HANGING—*also see Noose and Rope* If we are **present at a hanging** in a dream, we are party to violence and perhaps need to reconsider our actions. If **we ourselves are being hanged** in a dream, we are being warned of some difficulty ahead.

HARNESS Like a halter, a harness indicates some form of control or restraint. It might be that we are actually being restrained by our own limitations, or that we are being controlled by external circumstances. To be **wearing a harness** often takes us back to periods in childhood when we were not allowed the freedom we would have liked.

HARP The harp as a musical instrument indicates the correct vibration that we need in order to create harmony in our life. We ourselves are very much in control of this, and since the harp is also a symbol of music, rhythm, and harmony, we often link back to our own basic selves.

HARVEST To dream about a harvest indicates that we are going to reap the rewards of previous care that we have taken.

HAY In previous times, for many, a hayfield represented fun, relaxation and irresponsibility. Nowadays it is more likely to represent irritation—as in hay fever—and an unknown quality. To dream about hay is probably to be looking at a practical aspect in ourselves, such as the ability to provide shelter and sustenance for others.

HEARSE To dream about a hearse indicates that we are probably recognizing that there is a time limit on ourselves or on a project with which we are connected. Often we need to come to terms with our feelings about death in order to understand ourselves.

HEARTH / FIREPLACE To dream about a hearth or fireplace is to recognize the need for security—both knowing that the home, our place of existence, is secure, and recognizing the security of the *inner* self, the interior feminine, which gives warmth and stability.

HELMET If a helmet is **being worn by someone else** in a dream, it may have the same symbolism as a mask in that it prevents the wearer from being seen. If it is being worn by the dreamer, it is a symbol of protection and preservation.

HERMIT Dreaming about a hermit might represent a kind of loneliness that prevents us from making relationships on a one-on-one basis.

HILL—*also see Mound* To be **on top of a hill**—and therefore high up—indicates that we are aware of our own expanded vision. We have made an effort to achieve something, are able to survey the results of what we have done, and assess the effect on our environment and the people around us. We have achieved things that we previously thought impossible, and are now able to undertake further work in light of the knowledge we have attained.

HISTORIC To have a dream set in the past is to link with the person we were at some previous time, and perhaps with outdated beliefs and ways of living.

HIVE To dream about **a hive** can represent the effort that is needed to be made to create fertility—or fertile situations—for ourselves. The hive can also represent protective motherhood.

HOLE A hole usually represents a difficult or tricky situation. It can also be a place where we hide or feel protected. To dream about **falling into a hole** indicates that we are perhaps getting in touch with our unconscious feelings, urges, and fears. To **walk around a hole** suggests we might need to get around a difficult situation. We may also need to become aware of the other parts of ourselves that are buried beneath our surface awareness.

HOME Human beings have certain basic needs, such as shelter, warmth, and nourishment. The home, and particularly the parental home, can stand for all of these things. To dream about **being at home** signifies a return to the basic standards we learned as a child.

HONEY Honey almost inevitably represents pleasure and sweetness. To dream about honey—and particularly **eating it**—can be to recognize that we need to give ourselves pleasure. Equally, it can indicate that we have been through some kind of joyful experience that can now be readily assimilated as a part of ourselves.

HORSESHOE The horseshoe is viewed as a lucky symbol. Traditionally, if it is **turned upwards**, it represents the moon and protection from all aspects of evil. And if it is **turned downwards**, the power is reputed to "drain out," and it becomes unlucky. To dream about a horseshoe might also indicate that there will shortly be a wedding in your family or peer group.

HOOD A figure wearing a hood in a dream will often appear to be slightly menacing. Sometimes the hood can represent part of ourselves that is creating a problem—an aspect of our personality that might need to be uncovered in order for us to function in an acceptable fashion.

HOOK When we dream about a hook we generally understand that we have the ability to draw things toward ourselves that are either good or bad. It can also indicate that we are being hooked by someone, and not being allowed the freedom to which we feel we have a right.

HORNS—*also see Antlers* Horns appearing in dreams hark back to the idea of the animal in the human. The god Pan, who represents sexuality as well as life force, wore horns. A horn also represents the penis and masculinity. Because it is penetrative, it can also signify the desire to hurt. Protectiveness is also a quality of horns, since the male animal will use his horns to protect his territory. A **musical or hunting horn** suggests a summoning or a warning in dreams.

HOSPITAL—*also see Operation* Depending on our attitude to hospitals, when one appears in a dream it can represent a place of safety or a place where one is vulnerable. Seen as a **place of healing**, it represents the aspect of ourselves that knows when we need to allow ourselves to be cared for and nurtured. If we find **hospitals threatening**, it may be a sign that we have to "let go"—to put ourselves at the mercy of others and allow things to happen for us so a situation can be improved.

HOSTILITY When we experience **hostility inside ourselves** in a dream, it is a direct expression of that feeling. If, however, someone is being **hostile toward us**, it often means that we need to be aware that we are not acting appropriately, and that others may feel we are putting them in danger.

HOT Pleasurable feelings can be translated in dreams to a physical feeling. To dream about **being hot** indicates warm—or perhaps passionate—feelings. To be conscious of the fact that **our surroundings are hot** indicates that we are loved and cared for.

HOTEL Dreaming about being in a hotel or boarding house can mean that we don't feel secure in our current situation and that we might need to escape from it for a short time. Conversely, it can also mean that a situation we are in will only last for a limited time.

HOURGLASS To dream about something that measures time is often to alert us to the need for measuring our thoughts and activities. When the symbol is old-fashioned, like the hourglass, our perception of time and its management may, too, be old-fashioned. We need to use different, and more precise, ways of measuring those activities.

HOUSE A house nearly always refers to the soul, and the way we build our life. **Someone else in the house** suggests that the dreamer might be feeling threatened by an aspect of his or her own personality. If there are **different activities going on**, it indicates that there is a conflict between two parts of our personality—possibly the creative and the intellectual. **The front of the house** portrays the front that we show to the outside world. **Going into/out of the house**: we might have to decide whether we need to be more introverted or more extroverted. **An impressive, awe-inspiring house**: in a dream like this we are conscious of the Self or the Soul. **Moving to a larger house**: there is need for a change in our life, perhaps to achieve a more open way of life, or even more space. **Being outside the house**: the more public side of ourselves is being depicted. **A small house, or the house where the dreamer was born**: the dreamer is seeking security, or perhaps the safety of babyhood, without responsibility. **If the smallness of the house is constricting**: we are being trapped by our responsibilities and might need to escape. **Work on the house, such as building, repairing, etc.**: relationships might need to be worked on or repaired, or perhaps we need to look at health matters. We might need to take note of the damage or decay that has occurred in our life.

The different rooms and parts of houses in dreams indicate various aspects of our personality and experience. For example, dreaming about being in an **attic** has to do with past experiences and old memories. Interestingly, it can also highlight family patterns of behavior and attitudes that have been handed down. The **cellar** often represents the subconscious and the things we may have suppressed through an inability to handle them. A basement can also highlight the power that is available to us if we are willing to make use of it. We might not have come to terms with our sexuality, and prefer to keep it hidden. In dreams, a **bathroom** or toilet often reveals our attitude to personal hygiene and our most private thoughts and actions. The **bedroom** portrays a place of safety where we can relax and be as sensual as we wish. A **chimney**—both a passage from one state to another (ordinary to freedom) and a conductor of heat—can indicate how we deal with our inner emotions and warmth. A **hallway** can be illustrative of how we meet and relate to other people. And a **library** can be representative of our minds, and how we store the information we receive.

HUNGER Experiencing hunger in a dream indicates that our physical, emotional, or mental needs are not being met.

HUNT / HUNTSMAN Dreaming about **being hunted** usually has to do with one's sexuality. Its even older meaning is linked with death. By association, therefore, to dream about a hunt is to register the necessity for a change of state in everyday life.

I: Ice to Ivy

ICE When we dream about ice we are usually looking at emotions. We are aware that perhaps we are colder than we should be, shutting off any display of warmth and compassion. We are thereby enclosing ourselves in a situation from which it may be difficult to free ourselves.

ICE-CREAM To be **eating ice-cream** indicates that we may be accepting pleasure into our life in a way that we have not been able to do before. To be **giving other people ice-cream** indicates that we are giving other people pleasure.

ICICLES Icicles in dreams might make us aware that our environment is not supporting us in a way we would expect, which creates difficulties.

IGLOO An igloo in a dream stands for completeness and sanctuary, but also represents a cold exterior with a warm interior.

ILLNESS / SICKNESS To feel ill or sick in a dream is to identify a bad feeling; to vomit is to attempt to get rid of that bad feeling, situation, or relationship. Sometimes dreaming about illness can foretell *real* illness, but most of the time it represents the way we deal with difficulties of all kinds in life. It can mean that we are not putting ourselves in touch with the parts of ourselves that can help us overcome tough experiences and/or memories.

IMITATION To dream about **being imitated** is ambivalent. It could mean that we are aware that whatever we have done is the correct thing to do and that other people can learn from our example. It could also mean that other people are seeing us as leaders, when we ourselves do not necessarily feel that it is the correct role for us.

IMMERSION To dream about being **immersed** in water generally indicates that we are attempting to find the more innocent part of ourselves that does not need to be affected by external circumstances, and that we are attempting to cleanse ourselves, perhaps of ideas and attitudes that have been suggested to us by other people.

IMMOBILITY / PARALYSIS When immobility or paralysis is experienced in a dream, we are likely to be experiencing great fear or suppression. It usually indicates that the dreamer needs to literally sit still in their everyday life in order to achieve a kind of stillness that, while initially frightening, will soon become a state of peace and tranquility.

INAUGURATION To dream that we are being giving the honor of being inaugurated into something means that we can receive public acclaim.

INCOME The income we earn is an important part of our support structure, so any dream connected to it tends to signify our attitude toward our wants and needs. To dream about an **increased income** shows that we feel we have overcome an obstacle in ourselves and can accept that we have value. A **drop in income** signifies our neediness and perhaps our attitude toward poverty.

INDIGESTION To be **suffering from indigestion** in a dream shows that there's something that is not being tolerated very well. It could also indicate that we are actually suffering from indigestion.

INFECTION Dreaming about having an infection suggests that we might have internalized the negative attitudes of other people. Depending on where in the body the infection appears, there is information as to the type of "infection." For example, an **infection in the leg** might indicate that we feel we are being prevented from moving forward quickly enough in waking life.

INJECTION To dream about **being given an injection** is to be feeling that one's personal space has been penetrated. Other people's opinions, needs, or desires might be forced on the dreamer, leaving him or her no choice but to cooperate. To dream about **giving an injection** suggests that we are attempting to force ourselves on other people, which may have sexual connotations.

INJURED / IMPAIRED Dreaming about being injured or impaired suggests a loss of confidence and strength. If **we ourselves are injured** in the dream there can be a fear of moving forward into the future.

INSECTS—*also see Bee, Fly ...* Insects in dreams can reflect the feeling that something is irritating or bugging us. It might also indicate our feeling of insignificance and powerlessness. It will depend on the particular insect in the dream as to the interpretation. Thus, a **wasp** might indicate danger, whereas a **beetle** could mean either dirt or protection.

INSCRIPTION An inscription in a dream is information that will need to be understood. **Reading an inscription** can suggest that something is understood already, whereas **not being able to read an inscription** suggests that more information is required in order to complete a task.

INTOXICATION—*also see Alcohol, Drunk and Drugs* When we are intoxicated in a dream, it can be important to decide what has caused us to become intoxicated. **Being drunk** can indicate a loss of control, whereas a **change of state brought about by drugs** can represent a change in awareness.

INVENTOR Dreaming about an inventor or professor type links us to the creative side of ourselves. Usually this means the thinker rather than the doer: someone who is capable of taking an idea and making it tangible.

INVISIBLE **Becoming invisible** in a dream tends to indicate either that we are not ready to face the knowledge that understanding would bring us, or that there is something we would rather forget.

IRON When the metal **iron** appears in dreams, it usually represents our strengths and determination. It can also signify the rigidity of our emotions or beliefs, so we should consider being more flexible.

ISLAND Dreaming about an island signifies the loneliness one can feel through isolation, whether self-imposed or otherwise. An island can also represent safety in that, by isolating ourselves, we are not subject to external pressures.

IVORY Ivory is considered a precious and yet wholly unethically obtained substance. Thus, to dream about ivory is to be looking inside ourselves to discover what we are doing to obtain something precious—is it ethical?

IVY Dreaming about ivy harks back to the old idea of celebration and fun. It can also symbolize the clinging dependence that can develop in relationships.

J: Jailer to Justice

JAILER To dream about a jailer indicates restriction in some way, maybe by our own emotions or by somebody else's personality or actions. There will be a sense of self-criticism and alienation that makes it difficult to carry out our ordinary, everyday tasks.

JEWELS / JEWELRY Jewelry usually indicates that we have, or can have, something valuable in our life. **Being given jewelry** suggests that someone else values us; **giving jewelry** signifies that we feel we have something to offer other people. Jewelry can also indicate love given or received. When we are **looking for jewels** in a dream, we are attempting to find the parts of ourselves that we know will be of value in the future. **Counting or in some way assessing them** would suggest that a time of reflection is needed.

JOURNEY The image of a journey is a very potent one in dream work. Any time the idea of a journey becomes apparent, it has something to do with the way we move forward in life. A sense of having **completed a journey**—arriving home, touching down, and so on—indicates the successful completion of our aims. **Collisions** represent arguments and conflicts that are often caused by our own aggression. **A difficult journey behind us** means we have come through the setbacks of the past. **Obstacles ahead** indicate that we are aware of the difficulties that may occur and remind us to be aware that we often create our own problems. **Turning a corner** shows that we have accepted the need for a change of direction or made a major decision. **Avoiding an accident** means that we are able to control our impulses. **Stopping and starting** suggests that there is conflict between laziness and drive. **Being at a standstill/in a traffic jam** indicates that we are being prevented, or are preventing ourselves, from moving forward. This needs to be handled with care, since stopping might be appropriate. **Departing (departures from airports, stations, etc.)**: formerly, departures were interpreted as death. Nowadays the symbolism is much more of a new beginning—leaving the old life in order to undertake something new. When someone in our life leaves us, we might dream about departures and the grief that parting causes. In certain circumstances, to dream about **wanting to leave but not being able to** suggests that there is still further work to be done. To be **conscious of the time of departure** might suggest that we are aware of a time limit in an area of our life.

The destination, when it becomes apparent, will give us some idea of the goals we have. Our declared hopes and ideals might not correspond with those we subconsciously have—our inner motivation might be totally different from our outer behavior—and dreams will highlight this discrepancy. The exact nature of our objective is often not known to us until after we have confronted the obstacles along the way. It is often enough just to have a goal for that part of the journey.

Driving in dreams represents our basic urges, wants, and needs. If **we are driving**, we are in control. If **we are not happy when someone else is driving**, we might not trust that person, and might not want to be dependent on them. When **someone else takes over**, we are becoming passive. If we are **passing the car in front of us**, we are achieving success, but perhaps in a competitive way. When **we are being passed**, we might feel that someone has gotten the better of us. Once again, the way we are in everyday life is reflected in the dream. Our drives, aggressions, fears, and doubts are all reflected in our driving.

Passenger: if **we are a passenger** in a vehicle, we might feel that we are being carried along by circumstances and have not really planned our way forward. If **we are carrying passengers**, we might have knowingly or unknowingly made ourselves responsible for other people. **Travelling with one other passenger** suggests that we might be considering our relationship with that person.

The road in a dream suggests our way forward. Just as every vehicle demonstrates the dreamer's body and external way of being, the road reflects the way of doing. An **obstacle in the road** will reflect difficulties on the chosen path. **Any turns in the road** will suggest changes of direction. **Crossroads** will offer choices, whereas a **cul-de-sac** will signify a dead end. If a **particular stretch of road** is highlighted, it could indicate a particular period of time or a particular effort. **Going uphill** will suggest extra effort, while **going downhill** will suggest lack of control.

Traffic accidents and violations These might have to do with sexuality or self image; perhaps we are not being careful to ensure that our conduct is good. **A collision** might suggest a conflict with someone. **Road rage** would signify not being in control of our emotions and so on.

JUDGE When an authority figure appears in a dream, it is often harking back to our relationship with our father, with the need to be told what to do, or perhaps to have somebody who is more powerful than we are take control of our life. Since a judge upholds the law, it also has to do with our willingness to submit to authority on behalf of the Greater Good. In life, we learn to belong to groups, and to act in ways that are in keeping with the needs of those groups.

JUMPING **Jumping up** can represent attempting to attain something better for ourselves. **Jumping down** can mean going down into the unconscious and the parts of ourselves where we might feel we are in danger. And **jumping up and down** can indicate joy, and has the same significance as dance *(see Dance)*.

JUNGLE The jungle in dreams represents the eruption of urges and feelings from the unconscious. It can therefore indicate chaos—either positive or negative, depending on the circumstances. In myths, the jungle symbolizes an obstacle or barrier that has to be passed through in order to reach a new state of being. With this meaning, it has the same significance as an enchanted forest *(see Forest)*.

JURY When a jury appears in a dream, we are usually struggling with the issue of peer pressure. We might be afraid that others will not understand our actions, or that they could judge us and find us wanting.

JUSTICE—*also see Jury* Very often in a dream we do not seem to be capable of expressing our right to be heard, to articulate the things that we believe are correct. Therefore, to dream about either **justice or injustice** can indicate that the unconscious mind is trying to tell right from wrong. This is usually on a personal level, although it can have a wider implication as to what is morally right and the norm in society.

K: Kaleidoscope to Knot

KALEIDOSCOPE Just as a child is fascinated by the pattern that a kaleidoscope creates, so the dream image of a kaleidoscope can introduce us to creativity that can often become trapped.

KETTLE Because a kettle is such a mundane everyday object, to dream about one indicates our more practical, pragmatic side. If the kettle is unusual—such as an **old-fashioned copper kettle**—it denotes outworn, but still appreciated, beliefs.

KEY—*also see Lock and Prison* Keys often appear in dreams. They represent fresh attitudes, thoughts and feelings that are capable of unlocking memories, experiences, and knowledge that we have previously hidden. To dream about a **set of keys** suggests the need to open up all of our personality to new experiences.

KEYHOLE When we dream that we are **peeping through a keyhole**, we are conscious of the fact that our ability to see and understand is somehow impaired. Conventionally, a keyhole has been understood to represent the feminine, so that impairment could result from our attitude to the feminine.

KICK To dream about **kicking someone** often allows the expression of aggression in a way that wouldn't be acceptable in waking life. To dream about **being kicked** highlights a propensity to be a victim.

KIDNAP If we find ourselves **being kidnapped** in a dream, we are conscious of the fact that our own fears and doubts can make us victims. We are being overcome by our own "demons," which have ganged up on us and caused us to become insecure.

KILL To dream about **being killed** represents the dreamer being under an influence—usually external—that is making him, or an aspect of his personality, ineffective in everyday life. **Killing someone** in a dream is attempting to get rid of the influence they have over the dreamer.

KISS When we dream about kissing someone, it can suggest an acceptance of a new relationship with that person. Such an act can also signify that, on a subconscious level, we are seeking to develop a quality belonging to that other person in ourselves.

KITCHEN For most people, the kitchen represents the "heart" of the house. In dreams, it can often represent the mothering function, and therefore the place where many relationships are cemented and many exchanges take place.

KITE In Chinese lore, the kite symbolized the wind—and even today it represents freedom. So to dream about flying a kite can remind us of the carefree days of childhood, when we were without responsibility. Often the color is important *(see Color)*, as is the material from which it is made.

KNIFE—*also see Weapons* A cutting instrument in a dream usually signifies some kind of division. If we are **using a knife**, we might be freeing ourselves or trying to sever a relationship. If we are **being attacked with a knife**, it indicates that violent words or actions may be used against us.

KNIGHT A knight appearing in a dream, particularly a woman's dream, can have the obvious connotation of a romantic liaison—the knight in shining armor. This is actually a manifestation of her own inner masculinity and has to do with her search for perfection.

KNITTING The first symbolism connected with knitting is that of creating something new out of available material. A project or idea that is being worked on is beginning to come together. To **unravel knitting** in a dream suggests that a project that is being worked on needs to be reconsidered.

KNOB To be dreaming about a knob, such as a **doorknob**, can indicate some kind of turning point in one's life.

KNOCK To **hear knocking** in a dream generally alerts us to the fact that our attention needs to be refocused. For instance, we might be too introverted when in fact we need to be paying more attention to external matters.

KNOT If a knot is seen as a **tangle**, it can represent an unsolvable problem or difficulty, the answer to which can only be "teased out" gradually. Positively, a knot can represent the ties one has to family, friends, or work.

L: Label to Luggage

LABEL Often dreaming about labels links to the human need to name things. Our sense of identity comes from the name we are given, and our label has a lot to do with the way others see us and understand us.

LABOR **To be laboring** at something, in the sense of working hard, suggests that we have a goal we want to achieve. To dream about **hard labor** alerts us to an aspect of self-flagellation or self-punishment in what we are doing.

LABORATORY Dreaming about **working in a laboratory** indicates that we need to be more rational and scientific in our approach to life.

LABYRINTH / MAZE A labyrinth or maze appearing in a dream often signifies a confusion of ideas and feelings and/or the need to explore the hidden sides of our personality. With its many twists, turns, and potential blind alleys, a labyrinth is a potent representation of a human being, representative of meeting and overcoming difficulties in life that could impede progress. We often discover that, in attempting to find our way through the labyrinth, we learn a lot about ourselves after we get over the initial feelings of self-doubt and fear about which way to go.

LADDER A ladder in a dream suggests how secure we feel moving from one situation to another. We might need to make a considerable effort to reach a goal or take an opportunity. Often this dream occurs during career changes. If the **rungs are broken**, we can expect difficulty. If **someone else is carrying the ladder**, it could suggest that another person, perhaps a manager or colleague, has a part to play in our progression.

LAKE / LAGOON—*also see Water* A lagoon or lake represents our inner world of unconscious feeling and fantasy, which is a rich source of power when it can be accessed and understood. If **the lake is contaminated**, we have taken on ideas that are not necessarily good for us, whereas **a clear stretch of water** would indicate that we have clarified our feelings about ourselves.

LANDSCAPES The landscape in a dream can be an integral part of the interpretation. It usually mirrors feelings and concepts we have, and therefore reflects our personality. A **rocky landscape** would suggest problems, whereas a **gloomy landscape** might suggest pessimism and self-doubt. **A recurring scene** might be one where we felt safe in childhood, or could reflect a feeling or difficulty with which we have not been able to come to terms. Landscapes tend to reflect habitual feelings rather than momentary moods.

LANGUAGE Hearing a **foreign or strange language** in dreams illustrates some kind of communication, either from within or from the Collective Unconscious. It has not yet become clear enough for us to understand it.

LAUGH **Being laughed at** in dreams suggests that we may be afraid of being ridiculed, or may have done something we feel is embarrassing or inappropriate. It can also be seen as a sign of rejection.

LEAD (METAL) The conventional explanation of lead appearing in a dream is that we have a situation that is a burden to us. Maybe we're not coping with life the way we should be, and it is leaving us heavy-hearted. Lead, as in the **lead of a pencil**, has obvious connections with the life force and masculinity.

LEAD / LEADING (THE ACTION) **Leading someone** in a dream presupposes that we know what we are doing and where we are going. **Being led** suggests that we have allowed someone else to take control of a situation around us.

LEAF / LEAVES A leaf often represents a period of growth, and can also indicate time. **Green leaves** can suggest hope and new opportunities, or Spring. **Dead leaves** signify a period of sadness or barrenness.

LEAK—*also see Water* Dreaming about a leak suggests that we are wasting or losing energy in some way. If it is a **slow leak**, we are perhaps not aware of the drain on our energies. If it is **gushing**, we need to look at "repairing" the leak, perhaps by being more responsible in our actions.

LEASH Dreaming about a **dog leash** *(also see Harness)* would symbolize the connection between ourselves and our lesser nature. To **lose the dog leash** would indicate a loss of control.

LEATHER At its basic meaning, and depending upon the circumstances in the dreamer's life, leather can be associated with self-image. Often it is connected with protection, and subsequently uniform. For instance, a **motorcycle rider's leather suit** will make him or her easily identifiable, and will also protect in all types of weather. Dreams will often throw up an image that has to be considered very carefully.

LENDING If in a dream we are **lending an object** to someone, we are aware that the quality that object represents cannot be given away, that it is ours to have, but that we can share it. If **someone is lending us something**, then we are perhaps not responsible enough to possess what it represents on a full-time basis. Conversely, we may only need it for a short time.

LEPER To dream about a leper suggests that we are aware of some aspect of ourselves that we believe is unclean. We feel that we have been rejected by society without quite knowing why. We might also feel that we have been contaminated in some way.

LETTER—*also see Address* If we **receive a letter** in a dream, we might be aware of some problem with the person it is from. It is possible that the sender is known to be dead, in which case there are unresolved issues with that person or a situation connected with them. If we are **sending a letter**, we have information we believe might be relevant to that person.

LEVEL Usually a level surface suggests ease and comfort. Dreaming about **a road being level** would indicate that our path is fairly straightforward. **A level railroad crossing** suggests that we are approaching a barrier that requires our attention. We may not have enough information to take appropriate action.

LIBRARY—*also see House* A library in a dream can often represent the storehouse of our life's experience. It can also represent our intellect and the way we handle knowledge. A **well-ordered library** would suggest the ability to create order successfully. A more **chaotic, untidy one** would suggest that we have difficulty dealing with information.

LIFEBOAT Dreaming about a lifeboat could indicate that we have the feeling that we need to be rescued, possibly from our own stupidity or from circumstances beyond our control. If we are at **the helm of a lifeboat**, we are still in control of our life, but are perhaps aware that we need to offer assistance to someone else. Because the sea can represent deep emotion, in dreams a lifeboat may be helpful in handling our own emotions.

LIGHT A light, or lamp, in a dream generally means illumination, clarity of perception, confidence and optimism.

LIGHTHOUSE In dreams, a lighthouse tends to warn us of emotional difficulties. If we are **on land**, we are being warned of difficulties to come, probably from our own emotions. If **at sea**, we need to be careful not to create misunderstandings.

LIGHTNING Lightning in a dream denotes unexpected changes that may knock down the structures we have built as safeguards in our life. Alternatively, we may have to make changes in the way we think while leaving our everyday structure and relationships in place. Lightning can also indicate strong passion—such as love—that may strike suddenly but be devastating in its effect.

LILY Because of their association with funerals, for some people lilies can symbolize death. They can, however, also symbolize nobility and grace, and the interpretation needs to be carefully thought out. If we are **planting lilies**, we are hoping for a peaceful transition in some area of our life. If we are **gathering lilies**, particularly in **a woman's dream**, we are developing a peaceful existence.

LINE A line in a dream often marks a boundary or denotes a measurement. It can also signify a link between two objects to show a connection that is not immediately obvious. **A line of people** would suggest an imposed order for a particular purpose. If the dreamer is **waiting in line**, the purpose of the line will be important.

LINEN Linen in dreams, on a purely practical level, can suggest an appreciation of fine things. **Linen tablecloths**, for instance, might suggest some kind of a celebration in the sense of only using the best. **Linen bed sheets** might signify sensuality.

LION—*also see Animals* The lion in dreams signifies both cruelty and strength.

LIQUID Liquid in dreams can have more than one meaning. Because it is always associated with "flow," it can represent the idea of allowing feelings to flow. The color of the liquid in the dream *(see Color)* can also be important, since it can give an indication of which feelings and emotions are being dealt with. **Red** might represent anger, whereas **violet** might signify spiritual aspiration.

LOAF / LOAVES In dreams, loaves can represent our need for nourishment.

LOCK / LOCKED—*also see Key and Prison* A lock appearing in a dream might alert us to the fact that we need to free up emotions we've shut away. **To close a**

lock would suggest that we are attempting to shut something (perhaps a feeling) away, perhaps due to fear or possessiveness. Conversely, to **open a padlock** could mean we are trying to open up to new experiences. **To force a lock** would indicate that we need to work against our own inclinations to lock things away in order to be free of inhibitions. **To be fixing a lock** suggests that we feel our personal space has been trespassed on, and that we need to repair the damage.

LOCUST The image of a plague of locusts is so strong in Western thought that even in dreams it has come to represent retribution for some misdemeanor.

LOST To have **lost something** in a dream might mean that we have forgotten matters that could be important. This could be an opportunity, a friend, or a way of thought that has previously sustained us. To suffer loss suggests that part of ourselves, or our life, is dead, and we must learn to cope without it.

LOTTERY A lottery—particularly in today's climate—suggests the idea of gaining by taking a risk. To dream about **winning the lottery** would suggest that one has been lucky or smart in waking life. To dream about **losing** might suggest that someone else is in control of our destiny.

LUGGAGE Luggage in a dream can be slightly different from baggage in that luggage will symbolize something we feel is necessary for moving forward. It could be habits and emotions that have helped us in the past, and that can now be reappraised before being "repackaged."

M: Machine to Musical Instruments

MACHINE When a machine of any kind appears in a dream, it is often highlighting the body's automatic survival functions such as breathing, heartbeat and elimination. It usually has to do with some kind of mechanical, habitual form—that is, ordinary everyday things that take place. The "mechanics" of the body are an important part of our wellbeing, and often when we see a **machine breaking down** in a dream, it warns us that we need to be careful, that perhaps we are overstressing some part of our being.

MAGIC When we use magic in a dream, we are using our energy to accomplish something without effort or difficulty. We are capable of controlling the situation we're in, to make things happen for us and to create from our own needs and wants.

MAGNET We all have the ability to attract or repel others, and often a magnet appearing in a dream will highlight that ability. Since the magnet itself is inert, it is the power it has that is important. We often need to realize that the influence we have over other people comes not only from ourselves, but also from our interactions with them.

MAGNIFYING GLASS When anything is magnified in a dream, it's being brought to our attention. **To use a magnifying glass** in a dream indicates that we should be making what we are looking at conscious. It needs to be made part of our everyday life, and we have the power to create something out of the material we have.

MAKE-UP **If using make-up** in a dream it normally indicates our ability to change the impression we make on others. It can mean that there's a need to register the fact that we are covering up our features or, conversely, that we are enhancing our natural beauty. **If we are using cosmetics on someone else**, often we are helping them create a false—or perhaps better—impression.

MANURE Some of the experiences we go through can be painful or downright unwholesome. If we do not manage to understand what has happened to us, and make use of it as part of our growth process, we might find that those experiences remain in our subconscious and cause difficulty later. These bad experiences might appear as manure in a dream, alerting us to the fact that we should be breaking down our problems and making positive use of them.

MAP When a map appears in a dream, it often indicates a clarification of the direction we should be taking in life. We might feel that we are lost and need something to indicate the way forward, particularly where ambition or motivation is concerned. **A map that has already been used** by other people could therefore indicate that we are capable of taking directions, and learning from those people.

MARBLE Because it is a fine substance, marble appearing in a dream often indicates age or perhaps permanence.

MARKET / MARKETPLACE—*also see Shop* Dreaming that we are **in a market** indicates our ability to cope with everyday life, of being able to relate to people, and particularly to relate to crowds. It is also a place of buying and selling, and therefore often gives us an indication as to how we value our attributes, whether we have something to sell, or need to buy something.

MARRIAGE / WEDDING A marriage or wedding in a dream often indicates the uniting of two parts of the dreamer that need to come together in order to create a better whole. For instance, the intellect and feelings—or perhaps the practical and intuitive sides—might need to be united. Often, a marriage can be precognitive in that one may subconsciously be aware of a relationship between two people, but it has not yet registered on the conscious level. So, **to be attending a wedding** might indicate that one is aware of such a relationship. To be dreaming about **wearing a wedding dress** is to be trying to figure out one's feelings and hopes about relationships and weddings. To be **dressing someone else in a wedding gown** can indicate one's feelings of inferiority—"always the bridesmaid, never the bride."

MARSH / SWAMP When we dream about a marsh or swamp, it can indicate that we are feeling "bogged down" or overwhelmed. We feel that we are being held back in something that we want to do, and perhaps we lack the self-confidence or emotional support we need to move forward. A marsh or swamp can also indicate that we are being swamped by circumstances or trapped in some way by the circumstances around us. And to be **swamping someone else** in a dream might suggest that we are being too needy.

MARTYR Experiencing ourselves in dreams as **being a martyr** highlights our tendency to do things without being assertive enough to say no, and to act out of a sense of duty. When we are aware of **someone else being a martyr**, our expectations of that person might be too high.

MASK Most people have a façade they put on for others, especially at first. To dream about a mask often alerts us to our own or other people's facades. When we are not being true to ourselves, we often experience this in dreams as a "negative" or frightening mask.

MATTRESS—*also see Bed* Similar to a bed, to dream about a mattress indicates the feeling we have about a situation we have created in our life, whether it is comfortable or not. We are aware of our own basic needs, and are able to create relaxed feelings that allow us to express ourselves fully.

MEANDER In a dream, to have a path or road in front of you meandering—that is, not going in any particular direction—suggests that we often have to "go with the flow," and simply follow what happens without thinking much about the direction in which we are going. Sometimes the meandering has a purpose in the sense that, by moving around in an aimless way, we are actually finding out more about ourselves or the circumstances we're in.

MEDAL A medal is often a reward for good work or bravery, so when one appears in a dream, it is a recognition of our abilities. If we are **giving someone else a medal**, we are honoring that part of ourselves represented by the other person.

MEDICINE **To be taking medicine** in a dream suggests that on some level we are aware of part of ourselves that needs healing. Often we are aware of what the medicine is for, and are thus alerted to a health problem or to a situation that can be changed from the negative to the positive.

MEDITATION Interpreting the act of meditation in a dream will depend on whether the dreamer meditates in real life. In someone who does, it will suggest a discipline that is helpful to the dreamer, putting him or herself in touch with intuition and spiritual matters. In someone who does not meditate, it might indicate the need to be more introspective, in order to understand the need to be responsible for oneself.

MEDIUM Dreaming about **visiting a medium** often means that we are looking for some kind of contact with our own unconscious, or with the dead. We might also be attempting to alert our own intuition and use it differently from how we have in the past.

MELT To see **something melting** in a dream is an indication that our emotions might be softening. We are perhaps losing the rigidity we used to need in order to face the world. We are undergoing a change, and are becoming softer.

MEMORIAL To see a memorial, such as **a war memorial**, in a dream takes us back to a memory that might be "cast in stone." We need to be able to come to terms with this memory in order to move on.

MERMAID / MERMAN Traditionally, a mermaid or merman belongs to the sea as well as existing on land. This symbolically represents an ability to be deeply emotional and also entirely practical. Until these two separate parts are integrated, a human being cannot fully exist in either realm.

METAL Any metal appearing in a dream represents the restrictions of the real world. It can represent basic abilities and attributes, or hardness of feeling and emotional rigidity.

MICROSCOPE A microscope in a dream often indicates that we need to pay attention to detail. Also, we might need to be somewhat introspective to achieve a personal goal.

MILL / MILLSTONE A mill extracts what is useful from the crude material it is fed. It is this quality that is symbolized in dreams. We are able to extract from our experiences what is useful to us, and convert it into nourishment.

MINES—*also see Digging* Dreaming about mines signifies bringing the resources of the unconscious out into the light of day—we are able to use our potential. Interestingly, mines in dreams can also represent the workplace.

MIRROR—*also see Reflection* Dreaming about a mirror suggests concern about one's self-image. We are worried about what others think of us, and need self-examination in order to function. There might be some anxiety about aging or health.

MIST Mist is a symbol of loss and confusion—particularly emotionally—so when this image appears we might need to reconsider our actions.

MOAT A moat is a representation of our defenses against intimacy. In dreams, we can see for ourselves how we build or dig those enclosures.

MONEY—*also see Wealth* Money in dreams does not necessarily represent hard currency, but more the way in which we value ourselves. This symbol appearing in dreams could suggest that we need to assess that value more carefully, and be aware of what we "pay" for our actions and desires.

MONKEY To dream about monkeys or apes links with the mischievous side of ourselves.

MONSTER A monster appearing in a dream tends to be a fear of our own emotions or drives, personalized; whatever is worrying us appears as a creature.

MOON—*also see Planets* The moon has always represented the emotional and feminine self. It is the intuition, the psychic, love, and romance. To dream about the moon, therefore, is to be in touch with that dark, mysterious side of ourselves. Often in dreams the moon can also represent one's mother or the relationship with her.

MORTUARY When a mortuary appears in a dream, we are usually having to consider our fears and feelings about death.

MOTH A moth is largely associated with nighttime, and therefore connects to the hidden side of our nature. Also, because the moth can be self-destructive when there is light around, it tends to symbolize our dream self and the more transient side of our personality.

MOUND—*also see Hill* Traditionally, any mound appearing in a dream is supposed to link back to our early childhood needs, and the comfort our mother's breast brought.

MOUNTAIN In a dream, a mountain usually signifies an obstacle that needs to be overcome. By daring to **climb the mountain**, we challenge our inadequacies and free ourselves of fear. To **reach the top** is to achieve one's goal. To **fall down the mountain** indicates carelessness.

MOURNING—*also see Funeral and Weeping* The process of mourning is an important one in many ways. We not only mourn death but also the end of a relationship or a particular part of our life. Since it can sometimes be difficult to openly mourn or grieve in waking life, it will often appear in dreams as a form of relief or release.

MOVEMENT Movement in dreams is usually highlighted to make the dreamer aware of progress. **Moving forward** suggests an acceptance of one's abilities, whereas **moving backward** signifies withdrawal from a situation. **Moving sideways** would suggest a deliberate act of avoidance.

MOVIE To dream about being at a movie indicates that we are viewing an aspect of our own past or character that needs to be acknowledged in a different way. We are attempting to view ourselves objectively, or perhaps we might be escaping from reality.

MUD Mud in a dream suggests that we are feeling bogged down, perhaps by not figuring out practicality and emotion (earth and water). Mud can also represent past experiences, or our perception of them, which could hold us back.

MUMMY (EGYPTIAN) There's an obvious connection between Mummy and mommy, which is a play on words. In many ways our mother must "die," or rather, we must change our relationship with her, in order for us to survive. The Egyptian mummy in dreams can also symbolize our feelings about someone who has died.

MURDER / MURDERER We could be denying, or trying to control, a part of our nature that we do not trust. We might also have feelings about other people that can only be safely expressed in dreams. If we ourselves are **being murdered** in a dream, part of our life is completely out of balance and we are being destroyed by external circumstances.

MUSEUM A museum in a dream denotes old-fashioned thoughts, concepts and ideas. We might need to consider such things more objectively than subjectively.

MUSIC / RHYTHM—*also see Orchestra* Music and rhythm are expressions of our inner selves and our connection to life. To **hear music** in a dream suggests that we have the potential to make that basic association. Music can also represent a sensuous and sensual experience.

MUSICAL INSTRUMENTS—*also see Drum, Flute,*

Harp, Organ, Piano and Tambourine Musical instruments in a dream often stand for our skills and abilities in communication. **Wind instruments** tend to suggest the intellect. **Percussion instruments** suggest the basic rhythm of life.

N: Nail to Nuts

NAIL Dreaming about nails, as in **woodworking**, suggests our ability to bond things together. The holding power of the nail may also be significant. **Fingernails and toenails** usually suggest claws, or the capacity to hold on.

NAME Our name is the first thing we are conscious of possessing. It is our sense of self and of belonging. If we **hear our name called** in a dream, our attention is being directed specifically to the person we are. There is a suggestion that parents name their child so that the meaning of the name carries the biggest lesson the child has to learn in life. For instance, Charles means "man" and Bridget means "strength."

NARROW When we dream about something narrow, we are aware of restrictions and limitations. Sometimes we have created them ourselves; sometimes other people have created them for us. A **narrow road** could suggest some type of restriction, and is a warning not to deviate from our path.

NAUSEA Nausea in a dream usually indicates the need to get rid of something that's making us feel uncomfortable. It might be a reflection of our physical state, but since the stomach is the seat of the emotions, it could also represent an emotion that's distressing us.

NAVEL To be conscious of the navel, whether **our own or someone else's**, is to be aware of the way in which we connect our inner self with the outside world. It is the way in which a baby in the womb first becomes aware of its physicality. In dreams, we often need to be aware of our body image, which will help indicate the way we see ourselves and how we fit in to the everyday world.

NEAR When we are conscious of being near someone or something in a dream, we are on the verge of recognizing them in waking life. We might be becoming emotionally closer, or more able to handle whatever is happening.

NECKLACE — *also see Jewels* A necklace suggests a special object, and thus translates into special qualities or attributes. There is a richness to be acknowledged — either of feeling or of emotion.

NEEDLE In dreams, needles suggest irritations, but they can also signify the power to heal through penetration. A concept or knowledge has to be introduced from the outside; it might hurt, but it will ultimately make us better from the inside.

NEST The nest symbolizes safety and perhaps home life. We might be emotionally dependent on the people around us and afraid of "leaving the nest."

NET / NETWORK A net in dreams usually indicates that we are feeling trapped and entangled in a scheme or situation.

NEW Dreaming about something new suggests a new beginning, a new way of looking at or dealing with situations, or perhaps even a new relationship. Thus, **new shoes** might suggest a different way forward or a different way of connecting with the earth. A **new hat** might suggest a novel intellectual approach, whereas **new glasses might** indicate a fresh way of seeing things.

NEW YEAR To dream about the New Year is to recognize the need for a fresh start. It could also signify the measurement of time in a way that is acceptable, or a time when something can happen.

NEWSPAPER A newspaper in a dream normally suggests knowledge that is publicly available—perhaps information that we require in order to make sense of the world around us, or something specific to us. A **tabloid newspaper** might suggest sensational material, whereas **a broadsheet** would suggest better-researched data. **A Sunday paper** could suggest that we have the ability to assimilate the knowledge we need in periods of rest and relaxation. **A local newspaper** signifies that the facts we need are easily accessible.

NICHE / NOOK Everyone has a basic need to belong, and in dreams we are often conscious of finding our place in the world. This need manifests itself as a place where we are protected on all sides except from the front. It has been suggested that this is a return to childhood, prior to the age of four, when a child begins to realize that she or he is vulnerable from the rear. A niche or nook is therefore a place where we are safe.

NIGHT—*also see Time* Night signifies a period of rest and relaxation. It can, however, also suggest a time of chaos and difficulty. It is also a time that allows us to create a new beginning with the dawning of a new day. Used constructively, night is therefore the fallow period before fresh growth.

NO To be aware of saying "no" in a dream might be an important part of our growth process. We are capable of making decisions that go against the wishes of other people, without feeling that we are going to be punished. We are coming to terms with rejection and are no longer fearful. We are capable of standing on our own two feet.

NOOSE—*also see Hanging and Rope* A noose in a dream suggests that we have a fear of being trapped, perhaps by others' actions. We are aware that we can create a trap for ourselves, "putting a noose around our own neck."

NOURISHMENT / NURTURING—*also see Food* In dreams, symbols of nourishment are associated with basic needs. First, we require warmth and comfort; second, shelter and sustenance. Initially, we experience this as coming from our mother. Any dream in which we become aware of our needs links to our relationship with our mother. If our need for nourishment and nurturing is not met, we experience rejection and hurt. In dreams, the two are interchangeable.

NUCLEAR EXPLOSION To dream about a nuclear explosion can highlight our anxiety about big changes in our life. We do not know what effect that change may have. We do, however, know that we must undertake radical change.

NUDITY Freud assumed that dreaming about being nude was linked to sexuality. However, it has more to do with self-image. We have a desire to be seen for what we are, to reveal our essential personality without having to create a façade. To interpret a dream about **walking down the street naked** will depend on whether we are **seen by other people**. If we are seen by others, there might be something about ourselves that we want to reveal. If we are **alone**, we might simply want freedom of expression.

NUGGET More often than not, a nugget is made of gold and therefore signifies the best part of a situation. In dreams, we might find that a piece of information or knowledge represented by a nugget.

NUMBERS When numbers are drawn to our attention in dreams, they can have a personal or symbolic significance. Often the number will have personal meaning, such as a date or the address of a house where we lived. Our minds will often retain the significance of the number even though we might not consciously remember it.

NUT To dream about a metal nut, as in **nuts and bolts**, highlights our ability to construct our life in such a way that it will hold together. In the old-fashioned sense, a nut was considered to be feminine, and the screw masculine. Meanwhile, it was traditionally thought that **edible nuts** fed the brain, giving wisdom. They can still have this significance in dreams. Because of their shape, there is also a connection with masculine sexuality and fertility. To dream about nuts might suggest that we are trying to depersonalize issues about sexuality

O: Oar to Oyster

OAR The oar is a tool that enables a boat to move forward, but its use requires some skill. Thus it stands for our set of personal skills—those that help us "navigate" our life.

OASIS Most people see an oasis as a place of refuge in a desert. Because of its association with water, in dreams it becomes a place where we can receive whatever emotional refreshment we require.

OATS Oats in the form of **oatmeal** signify an almost "magical" food. Because they have been used since time immemorial as a staple food, they represent warmth and comfort.

OBEDIENCE When in dreams we **expect obedience from someone**, we are acknowledging our power and authority over others. To dream about having to be **obedient to others** indicates that we are aware of their greater authority and knowledge, and also of the disempowerment that has occurred.

OBELISK Any carved stone appearing in a dream suggests that we are considering how we have shaped our basic nature. The simpler it is, the more room we have for improvement; the more ornate it is, the more successful we are at using our creative energy.

OBLIGATION When we find ourselves **under an obligation** to one of our dream characters we are being reminded of our innate sense of duty. We might feel that we have done, or need to do, something for them that, in our heart of hearts, we don't think is appropriate.

OBSCENITY Often dreams will point to our lower selves, attributes we don't normally face in waking life. To have obscenity appear in a dream allows us to deal with these impulses safely, in a nonjudgmental way.

OBSESSION Obsession is an unnatural focus on a feeling, belief, or object, and may indicate that we need to take time to work through a difficulty. There is often anxiety about some past occasion or deed with which we have not been able, or allowed, to deal. When such an unnatural feeling appears in dreams, we can appreciate how harmful it can be.

OBSTACLE Obstacles in dreams can take many forms—a wall, a hill, a dark forest, etc. Largely, we are aware that these obstacles need to be overcome. How we do this in a dream can often suggest how to tackle a problem in everyday life.

OCCULT Occult actually means "hidden," so for someone to dream about the Occult when they have no knowledge of the subject usually suggests the need to come to terms with hidden fears. Most people tend to think of the Occult in its negative sense, as in black magic or Satanism, and thus may associate it with the egotistical side of their natures.

OCTOPUS Because the octopus has eight legs, it indicates that we can be drawn into something we find frightening and from which we cannot escape.

ODOR—*also see Perfume* Most other senses are sharpened in dreams, but the sense of smell is made available only if an interpretation is needed, so particular note should be taken of what we smell. A **pleasant smell** is likely to suggest good times, while a **bad smell** is likely to be a warning of unpleasant things.

OFFENSE **To take offense** in a dream is to allow a display of emotion and feeling about our sensitivity that may not be appropriate in waking life.
To offend someone in a dream is to recognize that we are not as aware of other people's feelings as we should be.

OFFICE Often our work or office situation gives an environment in dreams with which we feel comfortable. It is slightly more formal than our home, and often deals with our feelings about, or our relationship to, work and authority.

OFFICIAL / OFFICER To dream about an official or officer, unless we have a relationship with that person in real life, is to look at the part of ourselves that directs our life. Any official figure, particularly one in uniform *(see Uniform)*, alerts us to the part of our being that needs to belong to an organized group. On a conscious level we may rebel, but there is a part of ourselves that recognizes that we must fit in somehow.

OIL Interpretations will depend on which type of oil appears in the dream. **Cooking oil** can signify the removal of friction, or a way of combining different components. **Massage oil** suggests caring and pampering, whereas **engine oil** will highlight our ability to keep things moving.

OINTMENT Dreaming about an ointment means we need to be aware of the part of ourselves that needs to heal. The kind of ointment will often give information as to what we need. For instance, to dream about a **well-known brand** can suggest a nonspecific type of healing, whereas an ointment that has been **prepared just for the dreamer** suggests a more focused approach.

OLD / ANCIENT / ANTIQUE When we dream about old things, we are reaching into the past—perhaps to bring some kind of knowledge forward so we can make use of it in the present. Dreaming about **historical figures** usually means we are aware of qualities they possessed. Perhaps we need to develop those qualities in ourselves.

ONION—*also see Food* Oddly enough, an onion can appear in dreams and meditation as a symbol of wholeness—wholeness that is multilayered. **Peeling an onion** can suggest trying to find the best part of oneself or someone else. It might also show an attempt to understand the various facets of our personality.

OPERA **To attend** an opera in a dream suggests observing the "drama" of a situation around us (it might be more appropriate to observe than to take part). To **be taking part** in an opera, however, highlights our need for some kind of dramatic input into our life.

OPERATION—*also see Hospital* A dream about an operation can signify our awareness of our own fears of illness and pain, and also a recognition of our need to be healed.

OPTOMETRIST To **visit an optometrist** in a dream can indicate that we don't feel able to see a situation clearly, and that we therefore need help.

ORACLE Most of us like to know what's going to happen to us and like to be told what to do. So dreaming about an oracle connects us to the part of ourselves that knows what our next moves are. Often an oracle will appear as a person, such as a goddess or a wise old man. Or we can dream that we are using one of the many systems of prediction that are available in everyday life.

ORCHARD In dreams, an orchard might represent our attempts to take care of ourselves—it depends whether the trees bear flowers or fruit. If they have **flowers**, it will represent our potential for success; if they are **fruit** trees, we are being reassured about the harvest we may gather.

ORCHESTRA—*also see Music, Musical Instruments and Organist* We all have aspects of our personality that need to work in harmony in order for us to function. Dreaming about an orchestra represents ways in which we can bring those aspects together and make a coherent whole.

ORE Ore is a crude material that needs to be refined in order to be useful. In dreams, it can represent resources we have, although this may initially be rather crude. It can also represent new ideas, thoughts, and concepts that have not yet been totally understood.

ORGAN—*also see Musical Instruments* The **organs of the body** can represent different aspects of the self, both weaknesses and strengths. A **musical organ** will tend to highlight the dreamer's views and feelings about religion. In slang terms, the organ can also suggest the penis.

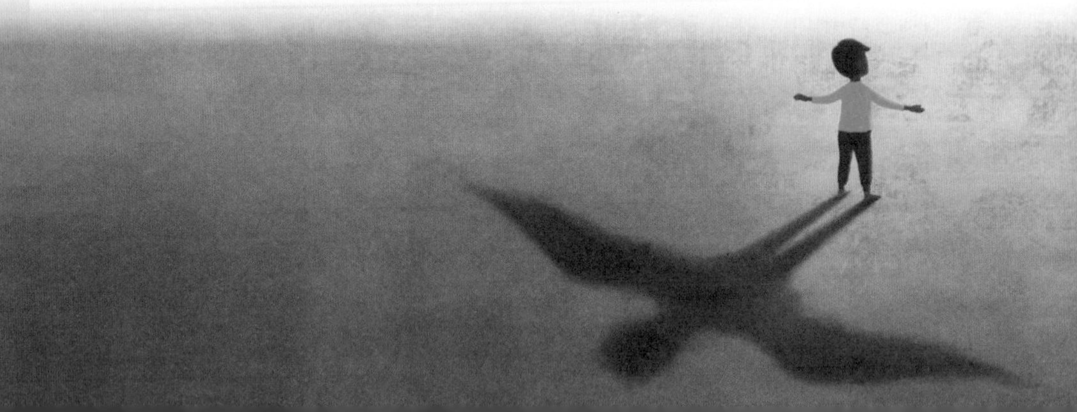

ORGANIST—*also see Orchestra* An organist represents the part of us that knows how to make use of the various vibrations of which we are formed. When we dream about this, we are appreciative of the fact that, as with an orchestra, we play in harmony.

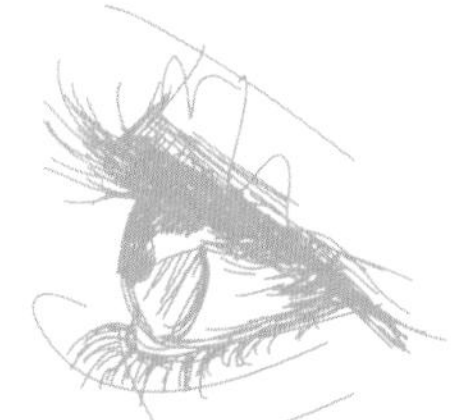

ORNAMENT Dreaming about **personal ornamentation** *(see Necklace and Jewels)* suggests an attempt to enhance something we have and value—whether qualities, feelings, or ideas—but want to make more valuable.

ORPHAN To dream about an orphan indicates that we might be feeling vulnerable, and possibly abandoned and unloved. If we are **taking care of an orphan**, we are attempting to heal a part of us that feels unloved. If we experience ourselves as **having been orphaned**, it could indicate that we need to be more independent and self-sufficient.

OSTEOPATH In dreams, an osteopath could signify our need to manipulate the circumstances of our life to a point where we are comfortable. Because an osteopath heals, for one to appear in a dream can suggest concern about health matters and how the body works.

OUIJA BOARD The use of a Ouija board can bring certain dangers. Dreaming about one might therefore be the psyche's way of alerting us to the dangers of exploring things we don't understand. It could, however, also denote being prepared to take risks, particularly with our peace of mind. When the **Ouija board seems frightening**, we are touching in on our deep fear of the unknown.

OUTLAW Inherent in the figure of the outlaw is someone who has gone against the laws of society. In dreams, therefore, the part of ourselves that feels beyond the law will appear as an outlaw. To **shoot an outlaw** in our dream is to attempt to control our wilder urges.

OVEN—*also see Baker* An oven represents the human ability to transform raw ingredients into something palatable. In dreams, therefore, it can suggest the ability to transform character traits and behavior from something coarse to something more refined.

OYSTER The oyster is reputed to be an aphrodisiac. In dreams it can therefore represent the sexual act or anything associated with sex.

P: Package to Pyramid

PACKAGE / PARCEL—*also see Address* When we **receive a package** in a dream, we are being shown something we have experienced but not explored. At this stage, we don't know what the potential of the gift is, but we can find out by exploring. When we are **sending a package or parcel**, we are sending our energy out into the world.

PACKING—*also see Padding* When we dream about packing suitcases in preparation for a journey, we are highlighting the need to prepare carefully for the next stage of our life. There is a need, or desire, to get away from past ideas and difficulties. To carefully pack a precious object indicates that we are aware of the intrinsic value to ourselves, or others, of what is represented by that object.

PADDING In dreams, our need for security can become more noticeable than we allow it to be in our everyday life. Because padding is protective material, we might need to be aware that we should *protect* ourselves rather than *defend* ourselves.

PAINTING **To paint** in a dream might alert us to creative talents (not necessarily painting!) that in waking life we don't realize we possess. **To look at paintings** in dreams indicates that we are questioning or paying attention to ideas of which we have not been consciously aware. **Painting the walls of our home** suggests that we are making recognizable changes to how we think and feel.

PAIRS The unconscious mind appears to sort information by comparing and contrasting. Particularly when we are aware of conflict in ourselves, we might dream in pairs (e.g. old/young, masculine/feminine, smart/stupid). It's almost as though there's some kind of internal pendulum that eventually allows the opposites to become a unified whole.

PALM To see a palm tree in a dream usually has to do with rest and relaxation.

PAN / POT In dreams, a pan or pot signifies nurturing and caring.

PANTRY—*also see Refrigerator* A pantry, being a repository for food, usually indicates sustenance or nurturing in a dream. What is in the pantry will determine the interpretation of the dream. In previous times, it would have referred to harvested food *(see Harvest)*, but it might be significant here if the dreamer registers that a certain food is missing.

PAPER Paper is one of those dream images whose meaning depends on the circumstances in the dreamer's life. For instance, in a **student's** life, paper would suggest the need to pay attention to their studies, whereas in a **mail carrier's** life it might indicate job anxieties. **Wrapping paper** could indicate the need for, or the possibility of, a celebration.

PARACHUTE Dreaming about a parachute suggests that, whatever is happening to us in real life, we have protection that will see us through. It might also indicate that we are able to face our anxieties and still succeed—at least in part.

PARADISE To dream about Paradise is to tap into the dreamer's innate ability to be perfect. We can experience total harmony within ourselves, and be totally innocent.

PARALYSIS—*see Immobility*

PARASITES Parasites such as **lice, fleas or bugs** in a dream mean we might be aware that someone is attempting to live off our energy in some way. Our lifestyle may, to them, appear to be exciting and more interesting than their own, or provide them with amusement.

PARTY When we are **attending a party** in a dream, we are often alerted to our social skills—or lack thereof. In waking life, we might be shy and dislike such gatherings, but in dreams we might cope well with the groups involved and have a greater feeling of belonging. To belong to a **political party** would indicate that we are prepared to stand up for our beliefs, and that we have made a commitment to a certain way of life.

PASSPORT In waking life, we might experience difficulty maintaining a good self-image, and in dreams we reassure ourselves by producing a passport.

PATH A path in a dream signifies the direction one has decided to take in life. The type of path, e.g. whether it is **smooth or rocky, winding or straight**, might be just as important as the path itself.

PAWN SHOP Dreaming about a pawn shop can indicate that we are not being sufficiently careful with our resources, either material or emotional. We might be taking risks that we need to consider more carefully.

PEDESTAL When we become conscious in a dream that something has been placed on a pedestal, we have obviously attempted to make that thing special. We have elevated it to a position of power.

PEN / PENCIL—*also see Ink* If a pen or pencil appears in a dream, we are expressing or recognizing the need to communicate with other people. **If the pen will not work**, we don't understand information we've been given. **If we can't find one**, we don't have enough information to proceed with some aspect of our life.

PEOPLE The people who appear in dreams are the characters with which we write our dream "plays." Often they appear as themselves, particularly if they are people we know or have a relationship with in the here and now. We might introduce them in order to highlight a certain quality or characteristic. We might also permit them into our dream scenarios as projections of our inner life or state of being. Finally, they might signify someone who is more important than the dreamer.

PERFUME—*also see Odor and Smell* When we dream about **smelling perfume**, we are often being reminded of certain memories. Smells can be extremely evocative, and we might need to recapture a certain emotion associated with that perfume.

PET—*also see Animals* Whereas in our waking state we might not be aware of our need for love and affection, when a pet appears in a dream we are reacting to our natural drive to give or receive love.

PHOTOGRAPHS When we dream about **looking at photographs**, we are often looking at an aspect of ourselves—perhaps our younger self or a part of ourselves that we no longer feel is valid. To be **given a photograph of oneself** would indicate that we need to take an objective view of a situation, or of ourselves in that situation. We need to stand back and look at what is going on.

PIANO A piano appearing in a dream is a symbol of our creativity. Just as in our everyday life we need to learn and practice playing the piano, we need to learn and practice using our creativity.

PICTURE In a dream, a picture is usually an illustration of something that's part of our life. The interpretation will depend on whether it is **painted**, or a **print of another picture**. For instance, in a dream, a **picture that we have painted** might have more emotional impact than an Old Master (an Old Master can also suggest our attitude to the past).

PILL For most people, taking a pill means doing something to make themselves feel better. In dreams, taking a pill might signify putting ourselves through an experience we need in order to improve our performance or potential. If we are **giving pills to someone else** in a dream, we might be aware that their needs are not being satisfied.

PILGRIM / PILGRIMAGE When we are **undertaking a pilgrimage** in a dream, we are recognizing the purposeful, directed side of our personality. We have a goal in life that might require faith to achieve.

PILLAR A pillar can be a phallic symbol, but it can also be about stability—the ability to stand firm in the presence of difficulty. In dreams, to find that we are a **pillar of the community** suggests that we should be taking more responsibility for our actions.

PILLOW In ordinary everyday life, a pillow or cushion can offer support or comfort. So in a dream, being conscious of a pillow might suggest such a need. Sometimes **what the pillow is made of** is important, and may have relevance in the interpretation of the dream. For instance, **a feather pillow** would suggest gentle support, whereas **a stone pillow** would represent a degree of rigidity.

PIMPLE To be overly conscious of something like a pimple in a dream is to suggest some worry about how one comes across to others. A pimple can also represent some kind of blemish in our character that will have to be dealt with.

PIN / STRAIGHT PIN It depends whether the pin is holding something together or is being used to pierce us, or an object, in our dream. If it is **holding something together**, it indicates the emotional connections or bonds we use. If it is **piercing an object**, a trauma is suggested, although it might be small.

PIN / BUTTON To have our attention drawn to a pin or button in a dream makes us aware of our right to belong to a group.

PINE CONE If a pine cone does not have a personal connection for the dreamer—such as a childhood memory—it will denote fecundity and good fortune.

PIPE On a purely practical level, a pipe can symbolize many things. A **water pipe** can give information about how we might handle our emotions (the size and type in this case will be significant). A **tobacco pipe** might suggest a means of escape, whereas a **musical pipe** indicates our connection to the rhythm of life.

PIT—*also see Abyss* Many people talk about the pit of despair and about feeling trapped in a situation. A pit in a dream makes us more conscious of this feeling. We might be in a situation we can't get out of, or find that if we are not careful we will put ourselves in such a situation. If **we are digging a pit** in the dream, we need to be conscious of the fact that we could be creating the situation ourselves. If **others are digging a pit**, we might feel we have no control over our circumstances, and that doom and disaster are inevitable.

PLACES When the environment or setting of a dream is particularly noticeable, there's usually some kind of message or information being given. Sometimes the place reflects our inner state of mind or mood; it might also be a reminder of a place that had meaning at some time in the dreamer's life, or of certain people.

PLAGUE To dream about a plague generally highlights some imbalance in ourselves. It could be something physical, emotional, mental, and/or spiritual by which we are overwhelmed, as happened with the plague of locusts chronicled in the Bible.

PLANETS To dream about planets is to connect to the subtle energies that surround us and have an effect on our life, even if not consciously.

PLANK—*also see Wood* To dream about **walking the plank** suggests taking an emotional risk. A plank of wood appearing in a dream can indicate that something needs to be repaired, or that we feel safer carrying our own means of support. If the plank is going to be **used in flooring**, the symbol is one of security, but if it is going to be used as a **door** or as a wall **decoration**, it signifies defense or adornment of one's inner space.

PLANTS—*also see Weeds* Because of the process of growth and decay that plants go through naturally, they are a symbol for progressive change. If the **plants in our dream are cultivated**, we should be aware of our ability to cultivate potential. If they **are dying**, we might have reached a stage where there is no more advantage in a certain situation.

PLATE A plate can be simple or ornate. In dreams, the interpretation will depend on this fact. A **simple** plate will indicate a need for simplicity in our life, whereas a more **ornate one** could suggest the need for celebration. If **we are holding the plate**, we are aware of what we have received from other people. If **someone else is giving us the plate**, they are offering us something that belongs to them, but that we can now share.

PLATEAU Many dreams will hold images of reaching a plateau. It can represent a period of peace and quiet, or stasis, where there is no energy left for change.

PLAY When in a dream we are **watching a play**, we need to figure out whether it is a drama, comedy or tragedy. This is because we often try to view our own life objectively. The **content of the play** could give us clues as to what our course of action should be in everyday life. If **people we know** are in the play we should be aware of the "drama" that we are playing out with them.

PLOWING As more people move away from working the land, this symbol becomes less relevant in dreams. It does mean, however, working on clearing oneself for new growth, and being able to prepare for change.

PLUMAGE Plumage being drawn to our attention in a dream can often stand for a display of power and strength. It might also be a signal of defiance; we need to stand firm and show our colors, as it were.

PLUMBING Dreaming about plumbing looks at the way we direct our emotions. It indicates how we use our emotions to bypass obstacles in order to create security for ourselves and control the flow of emotions within. Another interpretation is that of internal plumbing. Often, to dream about plumbing in this sense alerts us to something that's wrong inside our bodies.

PLUNGE To dream about plunging into something is to recognize that we are going into something unknown — and taking a risk. The risk will often take us into our emotional depths, and we will learn new things about ourselves of which we will be able to make use.

POCKET To dream about a pocket is to deal with one's personal secrets or thoughts — things we have *deliberately* chosen to hide. They may include thoughts about our abilities, and the value we have in our community.

POINT (SHAPE) Anything pointed normally refers to male sexuality, while to be aware of **the point of decision** is to resolve that action has to be taken in order for change to occur.

POINTING (THE ACTION) When we dream about **someone pointing**, we are normally having our attention drawn to a certain object, feeling, or even place. We need to take note of **who is pointing** it out to us, and **what they are pointing at**. We might feel that we are at the receiving end, which could make us feel that we are being accused of wrongdoing and need to look at the validity of our conduct.

POISON To recognize poison in a dream means that we need to avoid an attitude, emotion, or thought that will not be good for us; keep in mind that there is that which is not good for us *now*, and there is that which will not be good for us in the *future*.

POKER The presence of a poker in a dream links to masculinity, and also to rigidity. It can therefore suggest aggressive action, but also rigid attitudes and behavior.

POLE How the pole is being used in the dream will affect interpretation. It can be seen as an expression of life force, but also as a stabilizing force, a rallying point, or a support mechanism.

POOL—*also see Water* Dreaming about a pool highlights our need to understand our emotions and inner feelings. A **pool in the woods**, for instance, would suggest the ability to understand our need for peace and tranquility. An **urban swimming pool** might signify our need for structure in our relationships with others, whereas a **pool or puddle in the road** would suggest an emotional problem to be dealt with before carrying out our plans.

POPE Often, to meet the Pope in a dream is to meet the side of ourselves that has developed a code of behavior based on our religious beliefs. He might be benign or judgmental, depending on how the figure of the Pope was presented in childhood.

POSITION When a certain position is highlighted in a dream, it usually signifies our moral standpoint or our position in life. It can also give an indication of how we are handling situations in our life. For instance, something in the **wrong position** means we are going about things the wrong way.

POSTURES Body language is an important aspect in dreams. Our dream characters might develop exaggerated movements or postures to highlight information we need to recognize.

POVERTY To experience poverty in a dream highlights a sense of being deprived of the ability to satisfy our basic needs. We might feel inadequate, either emotionally or materially. Often we need to go back to basics to discover what our real needs are.

PRAYER Prayer suggests the idea that we need to seek outside help for ourselves. We might need someone else's authority to succeed in what we are doing.

PRECIPICE The fear of failure is often represented in dreams by a precipice. To **step off of a precipice** represents taking risks, since we do not know the outcome of our action. To try to **climb a precipice** is to make a tremendous effort to overcome obstacles that have arisen.

PREGNANCY Dreaming about pregnancy usually denotes a fairly protracted waiting period being necessary for something, possibly the completion of a project. A new area of our potential or personality might be developing. Interestingly enough, to dream about pregnancy seldom actually means one's own pregnancy, although it can indicate pregnancy in someone around us.

PRESENT / GIFT When a present appears in a dream, it can first of all be a play on words. We are being given a "here and now." We are being reminded to live in the moment, not the past or future. A present can also indicate a talent. If we are **receiving a present**, we are being loved, recognizing our abilities, and gaining from that relationship. If we are **giving a present**, we appreciate that we have characteristics that we are able to offer other people. **A pile of presents** in a dream can signify as yet unrecognized talents and skills. If the presents give some indication of time—e.g. birthday presents—we might expect some success around that time.

PRISON—*also see Key and Lock* Prison, in dreams, stands for the traps we create for ourselves in life. We might feel that outside circumstances are making life difficult, but in fact we often create those circumstances ourselves, whether on an emotional, material, or spiritual level.

PRIZE In dreams, **to win a prize** is to have succeeded in overcoming our own obstacles. We are also being acknowledged by other people for making the effort to succeed. **To give away prizes** suggests that we are giving public acknowledgment to efforts others have made.

PROCESSION A procession means an orderly approach, and often makes a statement of intent. In a dream, to see **a line of people** who all appear to have a similar goal or set of beliefs indicates that it is the intention of the group that is important. Often a procession is hierarchical, with the most important people first (or last). This could be important in a dream in enabling us to adopt priorities for ourselves.

PROPELLER A propeller in a dream acknowledges the drive and intent behind our progression. Recognizing our needs, we also need to understand how to move forward. The action of a propeller is to give us "lift," which suggests using the intellect.

PUDDLE—*also see Lake, Pool and Water* A puddle, being a smaller amount of liquid than either a pool or lake, can nevertheless have the same significance. When one appears in a dream, we are becoming aware of our emotions and the way we handle them.

PULLING If we encounter the act of pulling in a dream, it suggests a positive action. We are being alerted to the fact that we can do something about a situation. If we **are pulling**, we are making the decisions in a project. If we are being **pulled**, we might feel that we have to give in to outside pressures, so extra effort may be needed to make something happen. The object we're pulling, and the means by which we are pulling it, could be important. *(For examples, see Rope, etc.)*

PULSE A pulse is a rhythm that's essential to life. To be aware in sleep of one's pulse could indicate some kind of anxiety. In dreams, this could translate to a rhythm that is external. There might also be health worries.

PUNISHMENT When we feel that we're not conforming to what is expected, punishment or the threat of punishment is often present in dreams. Self-punishment occurs when we have not achieved our standards.

PUPPET When a puppet appears in a dream, there is perhaps a sense of being able to manipulate circumstances or people around us. A puppet can also represent the more mechanical processes of our being, the activities that go on automatically in the background.

PURSE A purse is normally used to hold money or something of value to us. In dreams, it therefore becomes something of value it its own right. **To find a purse** would suggest that we have found something of value, whereas **to lose a purse** suggests that we might be careless.

PUSHING When we are **being pushed** in a dream, there is an energy around us that enables us to achieve what we want. If **we are pushing**, then we are usually exerting our will positively. **Pushing something uphill**, such as a car or snowball, suggests that we are trying to resist natural forces.

PYRAMID On a physical level, a pyramid is a building of wonder. On a mental level, it is a structure of regeneration. On a spiritual level, it is a guardian of—and focus for—power. It will depend on the level of awareness in the dreamer as to which interpretation is valid.

Q: Quarantine to Quote

QUARANTINE Dreaming about having to **go into quarantine** signifies our inability to look after a vulnerable part of ourselves or others. It may also indicate our awareness of having to cut off the lower, more animal side of ourselves.

QUARREL To dream that we are **quarreling with someone** indicates an inner conflict. For a **man to be quarreling with a woman**, or **vice versa**, signifies a conflict between drive and intuition. To be **quarreling with authority**, e.g. police, indicates a conflict between right and wrong.

QUARTZ Quartz seen in dreams tends to represent the crystallization of ideas and feelings. It touches into our deep internal processes, often enabling us to express that which we have found impossible before.

QUARRY Dreaming about a quarry means quarrying the depths of one's personality—"digging out" the positive knowledge and perceptions we may have. Often dream symbols are created that link with childhood or past experiences that we may have buried and that now need to be brought into conscious understanding.

QUAY—*also see Journey* **Standing on a quayside** in a dream can indicate either moving forward into a new phase of life or leaving an old one behind. If **looking forward** with a sense of anticipation, it is the new phase that needs understanding. If **looking back**, there may be something in the past that needs attention before we can move on.

QUEST To be searching for something in a dream usually indicates that we are aware that we must undertake a frightening task in order to progress. Many mythological tales have as their main theme the search for something rare or magical (e.g. Jason and the Argonauts). Such themes can be translated into dreams in a personally applicable way.

QUESTION To be asking questions in a dream indicates a degree of self-doubt. To have **someone asking the dreamer questions** shows that the dreamer is aware that he has some knowledge to be shared. If the **question cannot be answered**, the dreamer may need to seek the answer himself in waking life.

QUESTIONNAIRE / QUIZ To be **answering a questionnaire or quiz** in a dream suggests that we may be making an attempt to change our circumstances without being certain of what we should actually do to bring about the change.

QUICKSAND Quicksand signifies a lack of security. In old-fashioned dream interpretation it represented business difficulties.

QUIET Becoming aware of **how quiet** it is in a dream shows that we need to cease being active for a while, perhaps in order to restore our emotional or spiritual balance.

QUILT The quilt or bedspread can often represent our need for security, warmth and love. To be aware of one in a dream, therefore, is our identification of that need. A particular quilt may have a special significance. For instance a **childhood quilt in an adult dream** would suggest the need for some kind of reassurance.

QUIVERING Quivering indicates a state of extreme emotion. Such a reaction in a dream would signify that we need to consider the emotion and deal with it in everyday life. For instance, an extreme fear reaction may be the residue of something that has happened to us previously and can only be dealt with in waking life.

QUOTE / QUOTATION To be giving a quote—as in **a building estimate**—can signify the value that we put on our services or talents. We may have difficulty with the accuracy—or the acceptance—of the quote and therefore, in waking life, will need to reconsider not only our own self-image, but also how we think others see us.

R: Rack to Rust

RACK A rack in a dream suggests a need for us to store something or to keep it in order. **A wine rack**, for instance, may mean that we have to pay close regard to our social life, whereas **a shoe rack** suggests a need to decide our best method of progress.

RADAR Radar in a dream represents our own personal intuitive faculty. It is our way of picking up subtle messages and signals that other people are giving out, often on a subliminal level.

RADIANCE When something appears as radiant in a dream it is being marked as having some kind of special quality that we may need to explore further.

RADIO As a method of communication, a radio suggests information that is available to everyone and therefore is widely understood. To dream about **hearing a radio playing** suggests a form of connection with the outside world. The context of the dream will give a wider explanation of the exact meaning.

RAFT A raft is a place of safety, often amid turbulence. While it may not be overly secure, it has the ability to support us. This is the kind of dream that occurs when we are dealing with emotional difficulties.

RAILWAY—*also see Journey* A railway in a dream signifies the way we wish to go in life. A **single track** suggests that there is only one way to go, whereas a **multiple track** suggests more opportunities.

RAIN In its simplest meaning, rain stands for tears and emotional release. We may have been depressed with no way to release our feelings in everyday life. Rain in dreams often becomes the first realization that we can let go.

RAINBOW A rainbow appearing in a dream is the promise of something better to come. The old story of the pot of gold at the end of the rainbow is so firmly entrenched in folklore that this meaning often comes across in dreams.

RAZOR It will depend on the type of razor which interpretation is given. A **cut-throat razor** would have the same symbolism as a knife—that is, cutting through the unnecessary. **A safety razor** suggests a less risky method is needed to enable us to reveal the truth about ourselves. An **electric razor** suggests that we need to pay attention to the image we put across in everyday life.

REACHING OUT Reaching out in a dream signifies our desire for something that we do not have. This may be either emotional or material. We may be trying to manipulate circumstances in such a way that others become aware of our needs.

READING—*also see Book* **Reading a book** in a dream suggests that we are seeking information. **Reading a letter** signifies receiving news. **Reading a list**—e.g. a shopping list—indicates a need to give some order to our life. **Reading a Bible** or other holy book is attempting to understand a belief system.

REFLECTION—*also see Mirror* A reflection seen in a dream has a great deal to do with the way we see ourselves at that particular moment. If the reflection is in a mirror, then our image will be perhaps more "solid," whereas one seen in water will be more transient. The story of Narcissus and the way he fell in love with himself (or rather his own image) is a warning to all of us against self-worship.

REFRIGERATOR—*also see Pantry* The refrigerator is a symbol of preservation. In dreams this becomes self-preservation and suggests that we may be turning cold emotionally or sexually. To dream about **rotten food in a refrigerator** suggests that we feel we may not be being sustained properly by those around us.

REINS—*also see Harness* In dreams, reins, as a form of restraint, indicate the need to control our own power and energy.

RELIGIOUS IMAGERY Religious images that appear in dreams introduce—or rather reintroduce—us to truths that we have long known to be. If spirituality is taken to be an inner truth, and religion as that which links us back to source, then it must be the case that religious imagery partly assists in that function of recognition. Using images that cannot be interpreted successfully in any other way reinforces the idea of spirituality being something separate in us. Because the images are so specific they may be startling.

RENT **Paying rent** in dreams is to undertake a personal responsibility. We are prepared to look after ourselves and to take responsibility for who we are. **Receiving rent** suggests that we have entered into a transaction that will benefit us.

REPTILES—*also see Animals* Reptiles in dreams link with our basic, instinctive responses. When there is a basic urge—such as a need for food, sex, etc.—we sometimes will symbolize it as a reptile.

RESCUE **Being rescued** in dreams is a powerful image, since it leaves us indebted to our rescuer. **Rescuing someone else** often suggests that we wish to have a relationship with that person.

RESIGN In dreams to resign is to give up. To dream about **resigning from work** means we are aware of major changes in our life. We perhaps need to look at our life and accustom ourselves to the idea that there are areas that we do not need to be in. **To be resigned** to something suggests that we have accepted the status quo in our life.

RESTAURANT Dreaming about a restaurant or cafe suggests a need for company. We may be fearful of being alone, but equally be afraid of allowing someone to delve too far into our private space. This public space allows for contact but, at the same time, we can control our own level of intimacy.

RICE—*also see Grain* Rice as an image in dreams suggests food, both for the mind and the body. It also suggests abundance.

RING A ring in a dream usually signifies a relationship of some kind. A **wedding ring** suggests a union and a promise. **A ring belonging to the family** would represent old traditions and values. **An engagement ring** suggests a more tentative promise of devotion. **An eternity ring** would be a long-term promise. **A signet ring** would indicate setting the seal on something. **A bull ring** suggests an element of cruelty.

RITUAL Rituals can range from the "sublime to the ridiculous." They are actions that are repeated over and over again in order to achieve a certain result.

RIVER—*see Water*

ROBE Dreaming about a robe, such as a **bath robe** can have two meanings. One is that of covering up vulnerability and the other is of being relaxed and at ease. The dream will indicate the correct significance. To be **dressing someone else in a robe** is to protect them.

ROCK To dream about rock suggests stability in the real world. If we are on **firm ground** we can survive. We may also be aware that we must be firm and stand "rock-like" and not be dissuaded from our purpose. **Seaside rock** can remind us of happier, more carefree times.

ROCKET The rocket in basic terms has a connection with male sexuality. To be **given a rocket** suggests recognizing that we are not functioning with the energy that we need. To **take off like a rocket** means moving very fast in terms of some project we have.

ROCKING Rocking in dreams can be a comforting activity and can put us in touch with the natural rhythms of life.

ROOF To concentrate on, or be aware of, the roof of a building in a dream is to acknowledge the shelter and protection it affords. If **the roof leaks** then we are open to emotional attacks. If we are **on the roof** we are not being protected.

ROOSTER The rooster has always been a symbol of a new day, and of vigilance or watchfulness, so to have one appear in a dream forecasts a new beginning or warning to be vigilant in one's daily work.

ROPE—*also see Hanging and Noose* A rope can suggest strength and power, though the power can turn against us. A **rope and pulley** suggests using the forces of weight to help us. If the rope is made of an unusual substance, **such as hair or material**, there is a special bond or necessity that requires the qualities the substance has.

ROSE / ROSETTE The rose in dreams has a great deal of symbolism. It represents love and admiration, and can also suggest fertility and virginity.

ROUND TABLE A round table in a dream is a symbol of wholeness. Partly because of the tales of King Arthur, there are various myths associated with a round table, but essentially it indicates that everyone is equal.

RUINS When **something is in ruins** we have to discover if it is through neglect or vandalism. If the former, the suggestion is that we need to pull things together. If the latter, we need to look at how we are making ourselves vulnerable.

RUNNING To be running in a dream suggests speed and flow. To be **running forwards** suggests confidence and ability. To be **running away from** signifies fear and an inability to do something.

RUSH To be in a rush suggests that we are having to contend with pressures. The pressure would be on our time, so it is interesting that rushes or reeds symbolize time.

RUST Rust represents neglect and negligence. We have not looked after the quality of our life properly and should look to address this oversight.

S: Sackcloth to Sword

SACKCLOTH In its oldest form, sackcloth represented humiliation. People were dressed in sackcloth to signify that they were less than dust. Nowadays in dreams it is much more likely to represent that we have humiliated ourselves in an action that we have taken.

SACRIFICES Sacrifice can mean to give something up and also to make something sacred or holy. So when those two things are possible within a dream scenario the dreamer is prepared to give up the ego for the sake of something greater or more important. Often a sacrifice is made because of passionately held beliefs.

SADDLE A saddle appearing in a dream will often indicate a need to exercise control over someone.

SAILING—*also see Journey* When we dream about sailing, we are highlighting how we feel that we are handling our life. We can either work with the currents or against them. If we are sailing **in a yacht** there is more of a sense of immediacy than if we were **sailing in a liner**. The first has more to do with one-on-one relationships, whereas the second suggests more of a group effort.

SAILS—*also see Sailing and Wind* Sails suggest the idea of making use of available power. Often the type of sail will be relevant. **Old-fashioned sails** would suggest out-of-date methods, whereas **racing sails** might suggest the use of modern technology. The color of the sails may also be important *(see Color)*.

SAILOR Most people have a rather antiquated idea of the sailor. It is this image that usually appears in dreams. They represent freedom, both of movement and of spirit. It suggests someone who is totally in control of their own destiny. A **modern-day sailor** has the added benefit of being in control of the ship.

SALAD Most food in dreams links with our need and ability to nurture ourselves and others. may be short of some kind of nutrient or stimulus and the dream state has alerted us to this.

SALMON The salmon signifies abundance and masculinity and is phallic. In its fight to mate by swimming upstream it can also symbolize the sperm. Often a salmon can appear **in a woman's dream** as a symbol of her wish for pregnancy.

SALT In dreams, salt highlights the subtle qualities that we bring to our life, the things we do to enhance our lifestyle. It has been suggested that if the water was removed from the human body there would be enough minerals and salt left to cover a fifty pence piece. We run most of our life through our emotions but the more subtle aspects are just as important.

SAND Sand in a dream suggests instability and lack of security. When **sand and sea are seen together** we are demonstrating a lack of emotional security. When the

sands are shifting we are probably unable to decide what we require in life. If we are conscious of the **sand in an hourglass** we are conscious of time running out.

SAP Sap in a dream means that we may be ready to undertake new work or a new relationship. We are aware of our own vitality and strength and prepared to take on new challenges.

SAVINGS In dreams we often develop images with dual meanings. Our savings may represent resources, either material or emotional, that we have hidden away until such times as they are needed. They can also represent our sense of security and independence. To dream about **savings that we did not know we had** would suggest that we are able to summon up extra energy or time, perhaps by using material or information from the past. To dream about **making savings in the present** suggests that we may need to give consideration to how to succeed in the future. If we are **aware of our goal in making savings** we should perhaps make long-term plans.

SCAFFOLDING Scaffolding in a dream will usually indicate that there is some kind of temporary structure in our life. **A hang-man's scaffold** will suggest that a part of our life must come to an end. We may, for instance, be aware that we have offended against some of society's laws and beliefs, and must be punished. We also may need to look at our propensity to be a victim. If **scaffolding** appears in dreams we should decide whether it is there to help us build something new or whether we must repair the old. We need a temporary structure to help us reach the height we wish in either case. If we are **building new**, that structure will support us while we build, whereas if we are **repairing the old** it will support the previous structure while we make the necessary changes.

SCALES Scales in a dream suggest the necessity for balance and self-control. Without that balance we cannot make a sensible decision as to potential courses of action. We must "weigh up" all the possibilities. Scales will also suggest standards—for instance, standards of behavior—to which we are expected to adhere. We may be weighed and found wanting. If the **scales are unbalanced** in a dream we need to search our conscience and discover where we are not functioning properly.

SCAPEGOAT The word scapegoat comes from the sacrificing of a goat to appease the gods, and in dreams this symbol can be highly relevant. If in our dream **we are the scapegoat** for someone else's action then we are being turned into a victim. Other people may be trying to make us pay for their misdemeanors. If **we are making another person a scapegoat** then this indicates a blame shift, and that we are not taking responsibility for our own actions.

SCAR A scar in a dream suggests that there are old hurts that have not been fully dealt with. These may be mental and emotional as much as physical, and can remain unnoticed until we are reminded of them. Just as in physical injury there can be many kinds of scars, so there can also be in the other areas. We may, for instance, be left with a pattern of behavior that is irritating to other people, but without the clear connection given by the dream image, we are unable to understand it.

SCEPTER The scepter is representative of royal power and sovereignty. When it appears in dreams it is usually indicative of the fact that we have given someone authority over us. We have abdicated responsibility to the point that the inner self has to take over. The scepter also has the same symbolism as most rods, which is, of course, phallic.

SCHOOL—*also see Education and Teacher* School is an important part of everyone's life. In situations where we are learning new abilities or skills, the image of a school will often come up in dreams. It is also the place where we

experience associations that do not belong to the family, and can therefore suggest new ways of learning about relationships.

SCISSORS Scissors in dreams suggest the idea of cutting the non-essential out of our life. This may be feelings that we do not think are appropriate, emotions that we cannot handle, or mental trauma that needs to be excised. The type of scissors may also be important to the dreamer. **Kitchen scissors** would, for instance, be more utilitarian than **surgical scissors,** which would suggest the necessity to be more precise. Scissors can also suggest a sharp, hurtful tongue or cutting remarks.

SCROLL Nowadays, a scroll will represent an acknowledgment of a learning process—i.e. the scroll presented to graduating students. It will depend on the circumstances what the exact interpretation is. We are endorsing either our own knowledge or information which has been given to us, so that we can enhance our life.

SCYTHE / SICKLE—*also see Weapons* As a cutting instrument, dreaming about a scythe can suggest a need to cut out non-essential actions or beliefs in order to achieve a desired end. The ancient symbol of the sickle, or scythe, also represents mortality and death yet is rarely a sign of a physical death when it appears in a dream—rather the death of part of ourselves.

SEA / OCEAN—*see Water*

SEAL Historically, a **wax seal** confirmed authority and power. It was also a symbol of identity. Nowadays in dreams, it is much more likely to signify legality or correct moral action. In dreams, **the possession of a seal** gives us the authority to take responsibility for our own actions.

SEANCE Dreaming about being at a seance can suggest a need to explore the psychic side of our nature. Remembering that psychic means "being in touch with self," this can suggest being aware of our intuition.

SEARCHING To be searching in a dream is an attempt to find an answer to a problem. If we are **searching for someone** we may be conscious of our loneliness. If we are **searching for something** we may be aware of an unfulfilled need.

SEARCHLIGHT—*also see Light* A searchlight in a dream denotes focused attention and concentration.

SEASONS When we become conscious of the seasons of the year in dreams, we are also linking with the various periods of our life (**Spring** signifies childhood, **Summer**—young adulthood, **Autumn**—middle age, **Winter**—old age).

SEED A seed in dreams stands for our potential. We may have an idea that is only just beginning, or a project that needs nurturing. **In a woman's dream** a seed may suggest pregnancy.

SHAMPOO Shampoo in dreams has an obvious connection with cleansing and washing. On a practical level, we are trying to "clear our heads" in order to think or see clearly.

SHAPES The number of sides that shapes in dreams have will be significant, as will the colors *(see Colors)*. At a certain stage of development, the geometric shapes that will give the individual a greater understanding of the abstract world begin to appear in dreams. It is as though the old perception of form is beginning to take on a new meaning and interpretation.

SHARK To dream about a shark may indicate that we are being attacked unfairly; someone is trying to take something that is rightfully ours. Being in **a sea of sharks** suggests that we are in a situation where we do not trust anyone. To be **pursued by a shark** may suggest that we have put ourselves in danger and created a situation by entering someone else's territory.

SHAVE Shaving in a dream suggests removing an unwanted layer—a facade which has been created.

SHELLS In dreams, a shell represents the defenses we use in order to prevent ourselves from being hurt. We can create a hard shell in response to previous hurt, or a soft shell, which would indicate that we are still open to being hurt. The spiral convolutions on a shell have also often been associated with perfection and therefore plenty. Dreaming about such an object would therefore link with a primitive understanding of things that we can permit ourselves to have.

SHELTER Any shelter signifies protection. The human is aware of the need for a safe space, and this symbolism comes across in dreams quite strongly. The images used could be anything from a snail shell to an umbrella. Usually dreams about shelter highlight our needs or insecurities.

SHIELD A shield is a symbol of preservation. It can appear in dreams as a **warrior's shield**, or as a barrier between the dreamer and the rest of the world. If we are **shielding someone else**, then we need to be sure our actions are appropriate and supportive. If we are **being shielded**, we need to be clear as to whether we are erecting the shield or whether it is being erected for us.

SHIVER To be conscious of shivering in dreams can represent either a fear of conflict, or of coldness of emotion. There is also a **shiver of excitement**. We may, in waking life, be reaching a conclusion or coming to a peak of experience.

SHOP A shop in dreams signifies something we want or feel we need. If it is **a shop that we know**, then we are probably consciously aware of what we want from life. If it is an **unknown shop**, then we may have to search our minds for information. A **supermarket** would suggest we have to make a choice.

SHOT / SHOOTING—*also see Gun and Weapons* **To be shot** in a dream suggests an injury to one's feelings. In a **woman's dream** it can symbolize the sexual act—as much because her feelings are involved as for the masculine imagery. It could also indicate that we may feel that we are becoming victims or targets for other people's anger.

SHOVEL / SPADE A shovel in a dream will signify a need to dig into past experiences for information. We may need to uncover a past joy or trauma, or possibly even a learning experience. The type of spade or shovel will be of relevance. A **garden spade** would suggest being totally pragmatic, whereas a **fire shovel** would indicate a need to take care.

SHRINKING In dreams, **shrinking** is to have a desire to return to childhood, or to a smaller space in order to be looked after. In everyday life we may be aware of losing face or of feeling small and this can be translated in dreams as shrinking. **To see something—or somebody—shrink** can indicate that it is losing its—or their—power over us.

SIEVE The sieve in dreams is a symbol of the ability to make selections. This is in the sense of being able to separate the large from the small, good from the bad, etc.

SIGNATURE Our signature in a dream suggests that we have an appreciation of ourselves. We are prepared to recognize who we are and to make our mark in the world.

SILENCE Silence in a dream can suggest uneasiness and expectancy. There is a waiting for something to happen (or not happen). If **someone else is silent** when we expect them to speak, we are unsure as to how that part of ourselves which is represented by the other person will react in waking life.

SILVER On a practical level, silver appearing in a dream suggests finance or money. Silver is something of value that can be held in reserve against possible difficulty.

SING To **hear singing** in a dream is to link with the self-expression we all have. We are in touch with the flowing, feeling side of ourselves and others. **To be singing** is to be expressing our joy and love of life. If we are **singing alone**, we have learned to be skilled in our own right. To be **in a choir** suggests our ability to worship or express ourselves in a peer group. Obviously, if the dreamer is a singer in waking life, the interpretation will vary.

SINKING **To be sinking** in a dream suggests a loss of confidence. We may be in despair at something we have done, and feel hampered by the circumstances. **To see someone else sinking** would suggest that we are aware of a difficulty which perhaps needs our attention. We may feel we are losing ground within a relationship or situation. What we are sinking into could be important. To be **sinking in water** would suggest a particular emotion is threatening to engulf us. To be **sinking in sand or a bog** indicates that we feel there is no safe ground for us.

SIREN To hear a siren—as in an **ambulance or fire engine**—is to be warned of danger. For those old enough to remember, such a siren will evoke memories of war and destruction. In particular, the "all clear" will serve to relieve anxiety.

SIZE To be conscious of size in a dream highlights how we feel in relation to another person, project or object. **Big** might suggest important or threatening, whereas **small** might indicate vulnerability or something "less than" ourselves. Thus a big house would be an awareness of the expansion of oneself, whereas a small house would indicate an intensity of feeling.

SKELETON A skeleton in a dream suggests the "bare bones" of something, perhaps an idea or concept. **A skeleton in a cupboard** represents a past action or shame that we wish to hide. A **dancing skeleton** is an awareness of the life that we have lived or are living. To **dig up a skeleton** is to resurrect something that we have buried.

SKULL If a skull appears in a dream we may need to look at the rest of the dream in order to find out the symbolism. The **skull and cross-bones** could represent either a romantic appreciation of a pirate, or a symbol of danger. Since the skull is a representation of the head it can also symbolize intellectual ability or rather, lack of it.

SKY In dreams the sky can represent the mind. It can also signify our potential. **Floating or flying** in the sky can be ambivalent, since it can either mean trying to avoid the mundane, or exploring a different potential. If the sky is **dark** it may reflect our mood of gloominess; if it is **bright**, our mood of joy.

SMOKE / SMOKING—*also see Fire* Smoke in dreams suggests that there is a feeling of danger around, especially if we cannot locate the fire. If **we are smoking**, we are trying to control anxiety. If we smoke in real life, but recognize in dreams that we no longer do so, we have overcome a difficulty. If smokers give it up in everyday life, they are likely to still dream about it.

SNAIL The snail tends to represent vulnerability and slowness.

SNAKE A "slippery" person or situation may be present in one form or another—perhaps a situation where another person cannot be trusted, or one that the dreamer knows they cannot control.

SNOW—*also see Ice* Snow is a crystallization of water, and as such represents the crystallization of an idea or project. **When melting**, it can represent the softening of the heart.

SOAP Soap in dreams suggests the idea of being cleansed. We perhaps need to create an environment of cleanliness—both of physical cleanliness and appropriate behavior. Often in emerging sexual dreams soap can appear as an image of ejaculated semen.

SOWING Sowing—in the sense of **planting seed**—is a symbol which has certain basic images attached to it. It can signify the sexual act, as well as suggesting good husbandry. It can also represent the beginning of a new project.

SPACE In dreams, when we are aware of the space that we occupy we are in touch with our own potential. We may be aware that our personal space is being, or has been, penetrated. To be **"spaced out"** is to have widened our personal boundaries artificially through the use of stimuli.

SPARK A spark in a dream represents a beginning. Being aware of a spark is to be conscious of what is going to make things possible. From a physical perspective, it is a small thing which gives rise to a greater one.

SPEAR The spear has many meanings. It represents the masculine in dreams and is phallic. It is the life-giving force. To see a **warrior with a spear** is to recognize the aggressive male. To **put a spear in the ground** is to mark one's territory. If we are **throwing a spear** we perhaps need to be aware of our more primitive aspects.

SPEED Speed in dreams identifies an intensity of feelings that is not usually available in waking life. Because everything is happening too quickly, it engenders anxiety in the dreamer, which can create problems.

SPIDER There is a great deal of ambivalence in the image of the spider. On a very mundane level it is disliked, perhaps because of its scuttling movement but also because of its association with dirt. In dreams it can also suggest deviousness.

SPIRE To see a spire in a dream is to recognize a landmark. In previous times, people oriented themselves by churches. Now a pub tends to be a marker, but in dreams the spire still persists.

SPLINTER In dreams, a splinter can represent a minor irritation. It is something that has penetrated our defenses and is now making us uncomfortable. Splinters may represent painful words or ideas. We may be holding onto ideas that cause negative feelings.

SPRING Springtime in a dream can suggest new growth or opportunities. Perhaps there is a fresh start in a relationship. A **spring of water** suggests fresh energy, whereas a **bed spring** or other type of coil would indicate latent power for movement.

SPRINKLING Sprinkling as a symbol in dreams suggests an attempt to make a little go a long way. Perhaps we need to get the best out of situations around us, by putting a little effort into many things.

STAB—*also see Knife* **To be stabbed** in a dream indicates our ability to be hurt. **To stab someone** is, conversely, to be prepared to hurt. Since a stab wound is penetrative it obviously has connections with aggressive masculine sexuality, but also with the faculty of being able to get straight to the point.

STAFF A staff, in the sense of **a stick**, is a support mechanism; whereas staff—as in **office staff**—is a support system. Dreaming about either should clarify our attitude to the support we require in life. It is worthwhile noting that one is passive in its use (the stick) and one is active.

STAGE—*also see Theatre* To be **on stage** in a dream is to be making oneself visible. An **open-air stage** suggests communication with the masses rather than a selected audience. A **moving stage** signifies the need to keep moving, even while performing a role. If we are **members of the audience** we need to be aware of the plot of the play and how it may be relevant to us.

STATUE Dreaming about a statue is to be linking with the unresponsive, cold side of human nature. We may be worshiping or loving someone and not getting any response.

STEALING—*also see Thief* To dream about **stealing** suggests that we are taking something without permission. This may be love, money or opportunities. If someone **steals from us** we may feel cheated. If it is by

someone we know, then we need to work out how much we trust that person. If it is by **someone we don't know**, it is more likely to be a part of ourselves that we don't trust. If we are **in a gang of thieves**, then we should look at, and consider, the morals of the peer group we belong to.

STEAM Steam in dreams can suggest emotional pressure. We are passionate about something without necessarily knowing what it is.

STERILIZE To dream about **sterilizing something** suggests a need for cleansing at a deep level. We wish to get rid of hurts or traumas and are prepared to put in the effort to do so. "Sterilizing" a situation may be taking the emotion out of it.

STIFFNESS Stiffness in dreams would suggest some anxiety or tension is present. There is a holding back of energy that is causing rigidity.

STINGING NETTLE A stinging nettle in a dream suggests a difficult situation that will have to be avoided. There may be irritation, particularly if we are not interacting with others or with our environment. **A patch of stinging nettles** could also suggest difficulty in communication if we are in the middle of it; others around us may be using words or circumstances to hurt us.

STONE Dreaming about stone can suggest stability and durability, but also a loss of feeling. To be **carving stone** is to be attempting to create a lasting monument.

STORM—*also see Lightning and Thunder* In dreams a storm indicates a personal emotional outburst. We may feel we are being battered by events or emotions. It can also signify anger.

STRANGLE To dream about **strangling someone** is an attempt to stifle the emotions. To dream about **being strangled** is to be aware of our difficulty in speaking out about our emotions.

STRAW Straw in dreams highlights weakness and emptiness. Unless the image of straw appears in a countryside scene, we are probably aware of a passing phase, which has little meaning. A **straw house**—being a temporary structure—would suggest a state of impermanence is present in our life.

STREAM—*also see Water* Dreaming about a stream suggests the awareness of the flow of our emotions. To be **in a stream** suggests being in touch with one's sensuality.

STRING String appearing in dreams signifies some kind of binding, perhaps to make something secure. It may also represent trying to hold a situation together.

SUBMARINE A submarine in dreams indicates the depth of feeling that is accessible to us. Usually we are looking at the subconscious depths rather than the spiritual heights.

SUCKING To be conscious of sucking in a dream suggests a return to infantile behavior and emotional dependency. **Sucking a lollipop** alerts us to a need for oral satisfaction in the sense of comforting ourselves. **Sucking a finger** can suggest a physical need.

SUFFOCATING When we feel **we are suffocating** in a dream, it may be that our own fears are threatening to overwhelm us. It can also indicate that we are not in control of our own environment. To be **suffocating someone** may mean we are overpowering them in real life.

SUITCASE—*see Baggage and Luggage*

SUMMER To be aware in a dream that it is summer suggests that it is a happy, fruitful time in our life. We can look forward to success in projects we have around us. We have the ability to make the most of what we have done to date.

SUN—*also see Planets* The sun in dreams suggests warmth and conscious awareness. A **sunny day** suggests happiness. To be **drawn to the sun** indicates we are looking for enlightenment. In turning towards the sun, the sunflower could be said to be a symbol of obsession, but also of worship. With its many seeds it also represents fertility.

SWALLOWING Swallowing in a dream suggests we are taking something in. This could be knowledge or information. Dreaming about **swallowing one's pride** signifies the necessity for humility, whereas something being **hard to swallow** shows that we have a need to overcome an obstacle.

SWEEPING To dream about sweeping suggests being able to clear away outmoded attitudes and emotions. To be **sweeping up** suggests putting things in order.

SWIMMING—*also see Drowning and Immersion* Dreaming about swimming has much the same symbolism as immersion. To be **swimming upstream** would indicate that the dreamer is going against their own nature. **Swimming fish** can have the same symbolism as sperm, and therefore can indicate the desire for a child. Swimming in **clear water can** indicate being cleansed, whereas **dark water** could symbolize the possibility of depression.

SWORD—*also see Weapon* The sword in dreams invariably suggests a weapon of power. We may have the ability to create power and use energy properly through our beliefs.

T: Table to Twins

TABLE—*also see Furniture and Altar* A table being **a focus for meeting**, whether socially or professionally, is usually recognized in dreams as a symbol of decision-making. As **a place for a family rendezvous**, the dreamer may consider meals to be an important ritual. In business and professional terms, **the boardroom table** also has an element of ritual about it.

TADPOLE Dreaming about tadpoles links to an awareness of the simplicity of life. We are aware that there is growth, but either we, or someone else, has not yet reached full maturity.

TAIL To dream about a tail can signify some residue from the past, something that we still carry with us. This residual energy might be in need of exorcism from your life, if it is unhelpful to your life and progress.

TALISMAN A talisman is a protection against evil or difficulty. When one turns up in a dream, we are often aware of the fact that our own mental powers are not sufficient to protect us from fear and doubt. We are in need of external help.

TALKING To be conscious of **people talking** in a dream gives a sense of being in contact with our own ability to communicate. We are able to express clearly what we feel and think, whereas in waking life we may not feel confident.

TAME To dream about **taming an animal** indicates our ability to control or develop a relationship with the animal aspect of ourselves. To dream about **being tamed**, as though we ourselves were the animal, signifies the need for restraint in our life.

TANGLED Sometimes when we are confused in everyday life, we may dream about an object being **entangled with something** else. Often the way that we untangle the object indicates action we should take in waking moments.

TANK Dreaming about **a water tank** is putting ourselves in touch with our inner feelings and emotions. Dreaming about **a war tank** connects us with our own need to defend ourselves, but to be aggressive at the same time. Such a dream would indicate that we are feeling threatened in some way.

TAPE Dreaming about **a measuring tape** indicates our need to "measure" our life in some way. Perhaps we may need to consider how we communicate with, or "measure up" to, other people's expectations. Equally, **if we are doing the measuring** we may be trying to create order in our life.

TAR Dreaming about **tar on the road** would suggest the potential to be trapped as we progress. Dreaming about **tar on a beach**, however, might suggest that we had allowed our emotions to become contaminated in some way.

TARGET Aiming at a target in dreams would suggest we have a goal in mind. The goal would depend on the type of target. To be **shooting at a bull's eye** could be interpreted as a search for perfection. To be **aiming at a person** could suggest either hatred or sexual desire.

TASTE When something is not to our taste in a dream, it does not conform to our ideals and standards. To have a **bad taste** suggests that whatever is signified by what we are eating does not nourish us. To recognize that our **surroundings are in good taste** suggests an appreciation of beautiful things and a desire to create more beauty in your own waking life.

TATTOO On a physical level, a tattoo will stand for an aspect of individuality in the dreamer. He (or she) wishes to be seen as different.

TAX In dreams, having to **pay a tax** suggests some kind of penalty for living the way that we choose to live.

TAXI In a dream **calling a taxi** signifies recognizing the need to progress—to get somewhere. We cannot be successful without help, for which there may be a price.

TEA Tea as a commodity in a dream represents a unit of exchange, whereas tea as part of a **social occasion** suggests inter-communication.

TEACHER—*also see Education and School* For many people, a teacher is the first figure of authority that they meet outside the family. That person has a profound effect on the child, and the teacher is often dreamed about in later years. Teachers can also generate conflict if their expressed views are very different to those learned by the child at home.

TEARS Tears in dreams can indicate an emotional release and a cleansing. If **we are crying** we may not feel we are able to give way to emotion in everyday life, but can do so in the safe scenario of a dream. If we dream about **someone else in tears** we perhaps need to look at our own conduct to see if it is appropriate.

TEASING When we are **being teased** in a dream, we are becoming aware that our own behavior may not be appropriate. If we are **teasing someone** and pointing out their idiosyncrasies, we may actually be highlighting our own discrepancies.

TEETH Popularly, teeth are supposed to stand for aggressive sexuality—although more properly they signify the growth process towards sexual maturity. **Teeth falling or coming out easily** indicates we are aware of going through some form of transition, similar to that from childhood to maturity, or from maturity to old age. **If one is anxious about teeth dropping out**, it suggests there is a fear of getting old, or an anxiety about maturing.

TELEPHONE **Using a telephone** in a dream suggests the ability to make contact with other people and to impart information we feel they may need. This could actually be communicating with someone in our ordinary everyday life, or with a part of ourselves with which we are not totally in contact. **Being contacted by telephone** suggests there is information available to us that we do not already consciously know.

TELESCOPE Using a telescope in a dream suggests taking a closer look at something. A telescope enhances our view and makes it bigger and wider. We do need to make sure, however, that we are not taking a one-sided view of things.

TEMPLE—*also see Church* Often in dreams a temple can signify our own body. It is something to be treated with reverence and care. It has the same significance as a church since it is an object built to honor and pay respect to a god or gods.

TEMPTATION Temptation is a conflict between two different drives. For instance, in dreams we may experience a conflict between the need to go out into the world and the need to stay safe at home. Temptation is yielding to that which is easiest and not necessarily the best course of action.

TENANT To dream about **being a tenant** suggests that at some level we do not want to take responsibility for the way we choose to live. We do not want to be burdened by having full responsibility for our living space. **To have a tenant** signifies that we are prepared to have someone live in our space. This may be the type of dream that occurs as we are preparing to become involved in a full-time relationship.

TENT A tent in a dream would suggest that we feel we are on the move, and not able to settle and put down roots. Anywhere we settle is only going to be temporary.

TERROR Terror in a dream is often the result of unresolved fears and doubts. It is only by experiencing such a profoundly disturbing emotion that are we likely to make an attempt to confront those fears. If **someone else is terrified** in our dream we are in a position to do something about it, and need to work out what course of action should be taken.

TEXT A text is taken to mean a collection of words that have a certain specific meaning. For a text such as this to appear in a dream would signify the need for encouragement and perhaps wisdom.

THAW In dreams, to be conscious of a thaw is to note a change in our own emotional responses. We no longer have a need to be as emotionally distanced as previously.

THEATRE—*also see Stage* In dreams about the theatre it will depend which part of the theatre is highlighted. If it is **the stage**, then a situation that the dreamer is in at this particular moment is being drawn to his attention. If it is **the auditorium**, then his ability to listen is significant. The play we create in our dreams as an aspect of our life is particularly relevant. If we are **not involved in the action**, it indicates we are able to stand back and take an objective viewpoint.

THERMOMETER A thermometer in a dream will be representative of judging our warmth and feelings. We may be uncertain of how we come across to other people and need some kind of outside measurement. A **clinical thermometer** would portray our emotional warmth, whereas an **external thermometer** would suggest our intellectual abilities.

THIEF—*also see Stealing* Dreaming about a thief links with our fear of losing things, or of having them taken away. We may be afraid of losing love or possessions.

THIRST Dreaming about **being thirsty** suggests that we have an unsatisfied inner need; we may be emotionally at a low ebb and need something to give us a boost. Anything that gives us emotional satisfaction—whether short- or long-term—would suffice.

THISTLE To be conscious of thistles in a dream is to be aware of some discomfort in waking life. **A field of thistles** would suggest a difficult road ahead. **A single thistle** would indicate minor difficulties.

THORN To dream about **being pierced by a thorn or splinter** signifies that a minor difficulty has got through our defenses. If the **thorn draws blood**, we need to look at where we are vulnerable in our life.

THREAD Thread in dreams represents a line of thought or inquiry that we perhaps need to follow to its end. **Threading a needle** has an obvious sexual reference. It can also, because of the perceived difficulty in threading a needle, suggest incompetence in ways other than sexual.

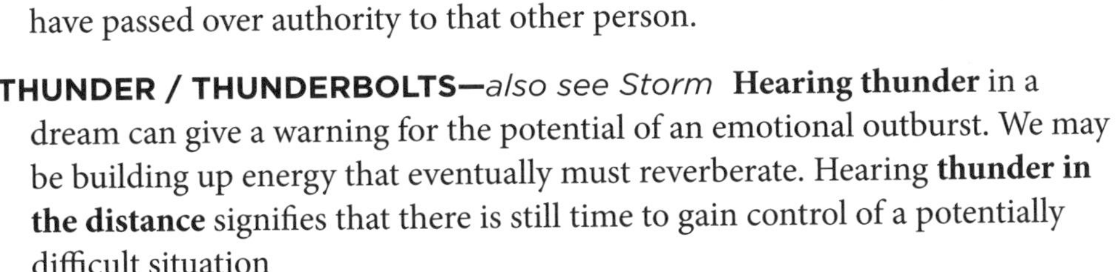

THRESHOLD Crossing the threshold in dreams indicates new experiences. To be **lifted across a threshold** may suggest marriage, or a new relationship.

THRONE When we dream about **sitting on a throne**, we are acknowledging our right to take authority. When the **throne is empty**, we are not prepared to accept the responsibility for who we are. It may be that we are conscious of a lack of parenting. When **someone else is on the throne**, we may have passed over authority to that other person.

THUNDER / THUNDERBOLTS—*also see Storm* **Hearing thunder** in a dream can give a warning for the potential of an emotional outburst. We may be building up energy that eventually must reverberate. Hearing **thunder in the distance** signifies that there is still time to gain control of a potentially difficult situation

TIARA—*also see Crown* A tiara, or diadem, in a dream often acknowledges the power of the feminine, or the ability to use the mental or intellectual abilities to obtain supremacy.

TICKET Generally, dreaming about a ticket suggests that there is a price to pay for something. A **bus or train ticket** might indicate that there is a price for moving forward,. A **ticket to the theatre or cinema** may suggest we need to take a back seat and be objective over a part of our life. Tickets to **a football or soccer game** might mean that we will have to pay for some area of conflict in our life.

TICKLING Dreaming about tickling can indicate that there may be a need for more humour when dealing with certain things—to break down our barriers of reserve.

TIDE Dreaming about a tide is about attempting to go with the ebb and flow of life—more specifically with the ebb and flow of our emotions. As a tide removes debris, the symbolism of cleansing is also relevant. A **high tide** may symbolize high energy, whereas a **low tide** would suggest a drain on our abilities or energy.

TILL There are two meanings of "till." One is to **till the ground**, and while that is a less potent images nowadays, the image still appears in dreams in the sense of cultivating opportunities. The other, more common meaning is as **a safe repository for money**.

TIME Usually the dreamer is only aware of the passage of time in a dream, or that a particular time is meaningful in the dream, if it is part of the dream scenario. The **daylight hours** suggest our conscious waking life. The **morning**: the first part of our life or our early experience is being highlighted. At **midday** we are fully and aware of our activities. The a**fternoon** is a time of life when we can put our experience to good use. The **evening** represents the end of our life, highlighting a time to be more relaxed. **Twilight** can indicate a period of transition and uncertainty insofar as our direction in life is concerned. And **night** can be a period of rest, introspection, secrecy and/or depression.

TOBACCO **If the dreamer is a smoker**, then tobacco, in a dream, is probably a comfort tool. **If not**, then the symbolism is probably more to do with the idea of using tobacco to achieve a particular state of mind. If the dreamer is **smoking a pipe**, there may be issues of masculinity to deal with.

TOMB **Going into a tomb** suggests going down into the darker parts of our own personality. We may be fearful to begin with, but later more at ease. Finding ourselves **in a tomb** suggests we are ready to face our fears of death and dying.

TOOLS Tools in dreams suggest the practical tools we have at our disposal for enhancing our lifestyle.

TORCH In dreams, a torch can represent self-confidence. It can also suggest the need to be able to move forward, but at the same time carry our own light.

TORNADO A tornado in a dream is a symbol of violent energy of one kind or another. Often it is emotions against which we feel powerless.

TORPEDO The torpedo has connections with masculine aggression. Its power in dreams can be destructive, but often is unconscious in origin.

TORTOISE The tortoise for most people suggests slowness but also perhaps thoroughness. It also in dreams signifies a shell, that perhaps we—or others round us—have put up in order to protect or defend ourselves.

TOTEM POLE In a dream a totem pole can link us back to a primitive need for protection by the spirits whose energy is powerful enough to be used by us.

TOUCH Touch in dream suggests making contact in some way. We are linking up with other people, usually to our mutual advantage. We are perhaps becoming conscious of both our need for other people and of their need for us.

TOURIST A tourist in a dream is someone who does not know his way around. If we are the tourist then we need to look at that aspect within ourselves. If someone else is the tourist then we need to be aware of what help we can give other people.

TOWER (obelisk, steeple, lighthouse, etc.) A tower in a dream usually represents something that we have developed in our life—whether an inner attitude or an outer life. While there are obvious shape-based connotations that connect it with masculinity, it is more correct to perceive it as the Self within a wider context. When thought of in this way attention can then be paid to other attributes of the tower, such as its doors, windows and overall shape. This leads to a greater understanding of the Spiritual Self. To dream about **a tower with no door** suggests that we are out of touch with our inner selves. **A tower with no windows** signifies that we are unable to see and appreciate either our external good points or our inner ones. An ivory tower suggests an innocent approach. A **square tower** signifies a practical approach to life, whereas a **round tower** is more spiritually geared. A **round tower at the end of a square building** is the combination of the practical and spiritual.

TOWN—*see City/Town*

TOY When there are toys in a dream we may be aware of children around us, or of the more innocent, playful and creative parts of ourselves. It can be a message from our subconscious that we are acting childishly.

TRAITOR To dream about a traitor suggests that one is subconsciously aware of deviousness. This may be in someone else, or it may be a part of our own personality that is letting us down.

TRANSFORMATION Dreams where things are transformed into something else suggests a shift in awareness. A landscape may change from dark to light (negativity to positivity), a person may change from masculine to feminine or one image may change into another. Once the dreamer understands the change is for the better, he is able to accomplish changes in his own life.

TRANSPARENCY When something is transparent in a dream we may be feeling vulnerable, but may also be aware of insights we would not normally have. **To be inside a transparent bubble**, for instance, would suggest visibility and vulnerability in our life, perhaps taking on new responsibilities. For someone else to be **behind a transparent shield** suggests that they are somewhat remote and unavailable to us.

TRAP / TRAPPED To be **in a trap** in a dream signifies that we feel we are trapped by outside circumstances. To be aware of **trapping something or someone** is attempting to hold onto them. To be **trapping a butterfly** is to be trying to capture the inner self.

TRAVELLING—*see Journey*

TREASURE Treasure in dreams always represents something that is of value to us. It is the result of personal achievement. To **find buried treasure** is to find something that we have lost, perhaps a part of our personality. To be **burying treasure** is to be trying to guard against problems in the future.

TREE—*also see Forest and Wood* The tree is symbolic in dreams of the basic structure of our inner life. When a tree appears in our dreams it is best to work with the image fairly extensively. A tree with **wide branches** would suggest a warm loving personality, whereas a **small close-leafed** tree would suggest an uptight personality. A **well-shaped** tree would suggest a well-ordered personality, whereas a **large, messy tree** would suggest a chaotic personality. There is a game that can be played in waking life if one dares. Ask a friend, a) what kind of tree does he or she think you are and, b) what kind of tree they think they are. The results are interesting. An oak for instance would represent strength.

TRESPASSING When we find **ourselves trespassing** in a dream, we are perhaps intruding on someone's personal space. This may also suggest that there is a part of ourselves that is private and feels vulnerable. We should respect those boundaries.

TRICKSTER When under stress this character can present himself in dreams as the character who points one in the wrong direction, answers questions with the wrong answers, etc.

TRIPLETS Triplets appearing in dreams suggest that events or situations should be looked at carefully in terms of physical wants, emotional needs and spiritual requirements. Then there would be development of spiritual stability.

TROPHY Dreaming about a trophy is to recognize that we have done something for which we can be rewarded. It depends on what the trophy is for as to its significance. The trophy will take on the significance of the object being presented. A **cup** would suggest receptivity *(see Cup)* and a **shield** *(see Shield)*, protection.

TRUMPET A trumpet in a dream will most often suggest either a warning or a "call to arms." From a practical point of view, it will be alerting us to some danger we have put ourselves in or are facing. When there is conflict around us, we may need some kind of warning to be ready for action and a trumpet can be one such symbol.

TRUNK In previous times to dream about a trunk was supposed to foretell a long journey. Nowadays, as people tend to travel light, it is much more likely to represent a repository for old things and hence signify old, outdated ideas.

TUG OF WAR To dream about a tug of war suggests a conflict between good and bad, male and female, positive and negative.

TUNNEL A tunnel in a dream usually represents the need to explore our own unconscious and things that we have left untouched.

TWEEZERS Dreaming about tweezers suggests that we need to look at a situation in minute detail. By grasping this detail, much good can be achieved.

TWINS In dreams twins may, if **known to us**, simply be themselves. If they are **not known to us** then they may represent two sides of one idea.

U: Ulcer to Unknown

ULCER An ulcer is a sore that is cured only with great difficulty. Thus, to dream about one makes us aware of work that needs to be done to heal a great hurt. It will depend on where the ulcer is as to what needs healing. To dream about a **stomach ulcer**, for instance, would suggest an emotional difficulty, whereas a **mouth ulcer** would suggest some problem with speech.

UMBILICAL CORD Often in life we can develop an emotional dependency on others, and the umbilical cord in dreams can signify that dependency. We have perhaps not yet learned to take care of our own needs in a mature way.

UMBRELLA An umbrella symbolizes the need for shelter and a sanctuary.

UNDERGROUND To dream about being underground will often allow us to come to terms with the hidden depths of our unconscious mind.

UNDRESSING When we find ourselves undressing in a dream, we may be putting ourselves in touch with our own sexual feelings. It may also be a sign that we need to freely and openly reveal our true feelings about a situation around us.

UNEMPLOYMENT Dreaming about being unemployed suggests that we are not making the best use of our talents, or that we feel our talents are not being recognized.

UNICORN—*see Animals and Fabulous Beasts* Traditionally, the only people who were allowed to tend unicorns were virgins. When a unicorn appears in a dream, we are therefore linking with the innocent, pure part of ourselves. This is the instinctive, receptive feminine principle.

UNIFORM—*also see Clothes* Dreaming about uniforms is all to do with our identification with a particular role or type of authority. However rebellious we may be, a part of us needs to conform to the ideas and beliefs of the social group to which we belong. Seeing ourselves in uniform confirms that belonging.

UNION Union indicates a joining together. **Union in pairs** suggests the reconciliation of opposites and the added energy this brings. A union, in the sense of a **trade union**, suggests collective action, which is for the good of all.

UNIVERSITY Dreaming about being in a university highlights our own individual learning potential. We may not be particularly academic in waking life, but may be subconsciously aware of our ability to connect together with people of like minds.

UNKNOWN The unknown in dreams is that which has been hidden from us, or that which we have deliberately made secret. This may be the "occult"—that is, knowledge that is only available to initiates. It may also be information that we do not normally need, except in times of stress.

V: Vacation to Vow

VACATION To be on vacation in a dream indicates a sense of relaxation and of satisfying one's own needs without having to take care of others.

VACCINATION In waking life, vaccination is an action that initially hurts but is ultimately good for us.

VALLEY Dreaming about **going into a valley** can have the same significance as going downstairs—that is, going down into the subconscious or unknown parts of ourselves. The result of this can be either gloominess or finding new areas of productiveness within us.

VAMPIRE When heavy demands are made on us, which we do not feel capable of meeting, a vampire can appear in a dream. We are figuratively being "sucked dry."

VARNISH Varnish is a protective outer covering designed to enhance the appearance of an object. Dreaming about varnish can therefore signify either covering something up to hide imperfections or protecting ourselves to present a better self-image.

VASE As a holder of beautiful or necessary things, any receptacle—whether a jar, vase, water pot, pitcher or urn—tends to represent the feminine within a dream. Such an object can also signify creativity.

VEGETATION Vegetation in a dream can often represent the obstacles that we put in front of ourselves in order to grow. For instance, **a patch of brambles** can suggest irritating snags to our movement forwards, whereas **nettles** might represent people actually trying to prevent progress. The image of vegetation also links with the forest *(see Forest)*.

VEIL When an object is veiled in a dream, there is some kind of secret that needs to be revealed. We may, as dreamers, be concealing something from ourselves, but we could also be being kept in ignorance by others.

VELVET It is usually the texture and quality that is relevant when a material appears in a dream. It is the sensuousness and softness of velvet that is significant.

VICE Dreaming about a vice in the form of a tool that clamps may suggest that we are being constrained in some way. And dreaming about a vice in the form of a wrong action indicates that we are aware of the rebellious side of ourselves that is out of step with society. We may in both cases need to make adjustments in our behavior.

VICTIM In dreams we are often aware of something happening to us over which we have no control. We are the victim—in the sense that we are passive or powerless within the situation. Sometimes we are aware that we are treating others incorrectly. We are making them victims of our own internal aggression, and not handling ourselves properly in waking life.

VICTORY There are many ways to achieve victory in dreams. The dream scenario may be a conflict between two aspects of ourselves or require us to overcome some difficulty. The sense of achievement we feel in dreams can be a feeling we can reproduce in waking life. It gives us confidence in our own abilities.

VILLAGE A village appearing in a dream suggests a tightly knit community. It may illustrate our ability to form supportive relationships and a community spirit.

VINE/VINEYARD A vine or vineyard in dreams can suggest growth and fruitfulness. This can be of one's whole self, or the various parts.

VINEGAR Vinegar, because it is sour, is a representation of all that is problematic in taking in information. It can thus signify knowledge that is unpalatable.

VIOLENCE Any violence in dreams is a reflection of our own inner feeling, sometimes about ourselves, sometimes about the situations around us. Often the type of violence is worthy of notice if we are fully to understand ourselves.

VIRGIN To dream about **being a virgin** suggests a state of innocence and purity. To dream that **someone else is a virgin** highlights the ideals of integrity and honesty.

VISIT To be **visited by someone** in a dream can suggest that there is information, warmth or love available to us. If it is **someone we know**, then this may apply in a real-life situation. If it is not, then there may be a facet of our personality which is trying to make itself apparent.

VITAMIN—*also see Pill* Dreaming about taking vitamins indicates that we have a concern about health. We may be aware that we are not nurturing ourselves properly and require additional help. We may sense that we are not being sufficiently nourished in our lives.

VOICE We all have an inner awareness of our own state that is sometimes difficult to express verbally. Often in dreams we are able to use our voices in more effective ways than in waking life. And sometimes we are **spoken to** in dreams so that we remember the information given.

VOLCANO The image of a volcano in dreams is a very telling one, partly because of its unpredictability. To dream about a **volcano being extinct** can indicate either that we have "killed off" our passions, or that a difficult situation has come to an end. This may be one that has been around for some time.

VOTE Dreaming about voting in an election, whether general or within the workplace, highlights our wish and ability to belong to groups. If we are conscious we are **voting with the group** we are happy to accept group practice. **Voting against the group** indicates a need to rebel.

VOUCHER A voucher—in the sense of a **promissory note**—can be taken in dreams to suggest our ability to give ourselves permission to do something. If, for instance, it is a **money-off voucher** we may not be valuing ourselves properly, or alternatively we could be looking for an easy option.

VOW A vow is a pact or agreement between two people or oneself and God. To dream about **making such a vow** is to be recognizing responsibility for one's own life. It is more solemn than a simple promise and the results are consequently more far-reaching.

W: Wading to Writing

WADING Dreaming about wading puts us in the position of recognizing what our emotions can do to us. If we are **impeded by the water** *(see Water)*, then we need to appreciate how our emotions can prevent us from moving forward. If we are **enjoying our wading experience,** then we may expect our connection with life to bring contentment. Sometimes the depths to which our bodies are immersed can give us information as to how we cope with external circumstances.

WAFER A wafer in a dream can represent something that is fragile, easily broken and that we therefore need to treat with care.

WAGES Wages are normally paid in exchange for work done. In dreams, to be **receiving wages** signifies that we have done a good job. To be **paying**

somebody wages implies that we owe that person something. To **receive a wage packet** suggests that our value is tied up with other things such as loyalty and duty.

WAILING Wailing is a long, protracted way of releasing emotions. When we hear **someone wailing** in a dream, we become conscious of someone else's sadness. When we **ourselves are wailing**, we may be allowing ourselves an emotional release that would not be seen to be appropriate in everyday life.

WAITING **To be waiting** for somebody, or something, in a dream implies a need to recognize a sense of anticipation. We may be looking to other people, or outside circumstances, to help us move forward or make decisions. If **we are impatient**, it may be that our expectations are too high. If we are **waiting patiently**, there is the understanding that events will happen in their own good time.

WAITER / WAITRESS If we are **in the role of waiter or waitress**, we are aware of our ability to care for other people. If **we are being waited on**, we perhaps need to be nurtured and made to feel special.

WAKE (FUNERAL) A wake, in the sense of a funeral service, gives us an opportunity to grieve properly. When in dreams we find ourselves attending such an occasion, we need to be aware that there may be some reason in our life for us to go through a period of grieving. We need to let go of that which we hold dear.

WAKING UP There is a condition in sleeping where we become alert to the fact that we are dreaming and that we can wake up. This appears partly as a way of forcing us into taking note of a particular action or circumstance, and partly to enable us to use, if we want to, the therapeutic tool of being able to awaken and make an adjustment that might have a happier ending.

WALKING In a dream, walking indicates the way in which we should be moving forward. To be **walking purposefully** suggests that we know where we are going. To be **wandering aimlessly** suggests that we need to create goals for ourselves. To take **pleasure in the act of walking** is to return to the innocence of the child. To be **using a walking stick** is to recognize our need for support and assistance from others.

WALLET In dreams, the wallet is a representation of where we keep our resources safe, both financial and all others.

WALLPAPER To be stripping wallpaper **in dreams suggests stripping away** the old facade in order to create a new image. **To be putting up wallpaper** signifies covering up the old self (possibly superficially), particularly if the old wallpaper is not removed.

WAND When we dream about **using a wand** we are aware of our influence over others. Conversely, if **someone else uses a wand** we are aware of the power of suggestion, either negative or positive.

WANT To be conscious of a want in a dream is perhaps to link with our basic nature. We may have suppressed those wants in waking life only to have them surface in dreams.

WAR In dreams war always denotes conflict, suggesting that we need to be more conscious of the effect our actions will have on others.

WARDEN A warden in a dream is often a manifestation of the part of our personality that acts as monitor or attempts to suppress other parts of our personality.

WAREHOUSE Being primarily a storage place, a warehouse in a dream has the symbolism of being a repository either for spiritual energy or spiritual rubbish.

WARMTH Warmth in a dream touches our "feel-good" factor and enhances our sense of comfort and well-being.

WARNING To receive a warning in a dream suggests that we are aware that either internally or externally something needs attention. We may be putting ourselves in danger.

WARRANT A warrant represents permission from a higher authority, either spiritual or physical. It will depend on the type of warrant as to what action the dreamer needs to take. For instance, **a search warrant** suggests looking at one's motives, whereas **a warrant for arrest** indicates we need to stop carrying out a particular action.

WARTS Any blemish that comes to our attention in dreams can be accepted as evidence of there being a distortion in our view of the world.

WASHING—*also see Water* Dreaming about **washing either oneself, or for instance, clothes,** suggests getting rid of negative feelings. We may need to change our attitude, either internally or externally. **Washing other people** touches on our need to care for others.

WASTE Waste in dreams signifies matter or information that we no longer need, so can now throw away. Waste can also suggest a misuse of resources; we may, initially, be using too much energy on a particular project, for example.

WATCHING In dreams, we are often conscious of the Self that is watching and participating in the dream. We need to be aware of all parts of the dream in order to achieve the best results.

WATER Water is usually taken in dreams to symbolize all that is emotional and feminine. It is a mysterious substance, given that it has the ability to flow through, over and around objects. It has the quality of being able to wear away anything that gets in its way. Water can also stand for the dreamer's potential and his ability to create a new life in response to his own inner urgings.

WATERFALL A waterfall at its basic level of interpretation can be taken to represent an orgasm. It can also signify any display of emotion that is forceful and yet somewhat controlled.

WAX Dreaming about wax is a great deal to do with the malleability that it is possible to achieve in our life. We should be prepared to give way, but also to be firm when necessary.

WEALTH—*also see Money* Dreaming about **being wealthy** is to dream about having the things that we need in abundance. We may have come though a period where we have put in a lot of effort, which means that to dream about having **a great deal of wealth** indicates that we have achieved what we have set out to do.

WEAPONS To dream about weapons usually suggests internalized aggression and/or a desire to hurt someone or something in some way. Depending on the weapon that we dream about we may get a fairly good idea of what the problem is in the waking self. An **arrow** indicates being pierced by some kind of powerful emotion—hurt by someone through words or actions and a need to turn our attention inwards in order to make ourselves feel better. The **gun or pistol** traditionally represents male sexuality and for **a woman to dream about being shot** often indicates her wish for, or fear of, sexual aggression. If **we are shooting the gun** ourselves we may be using our masculine abilities in quite an aggressive way, in order to defend ourselves. A **knife** represents the ability to cut through debris, to "cut into" whatever is bothering us and to cut out the hypocrisy that perhaps is prevailing in a situation. The **sword** has more than one meaning. Because of its hilt—which is a cross shape—it often represents a system of belief that is used in a powerful way. Equally, it can be used to suggest spiritual strength, creating an ability to cut away the unnecessary even more powerfully than the knife. The **sword when sheathed** is the soul or the Self in the body.

WEATHER Specific types of weather in a dream usually indicates our moods and emotions. We are very much aware of changing external situations and have to be careful to adjust our conduct in response to these.

WEAVING Weaving suggests the need to take responsibility for our own life. To be doing any handicraft shows that we have situations in hand.

WEB The appearance of a web in a dream may mean that we are caught up in a situation that could trap us—a "sticky" situation in which we don't quite know which direction to move. Because the situation is complex, we have no idea which way is going to be most advantageous for us.

WEDDING—*see Marriage*

WEEDS—*also see Plants* Weeds are unwanted **plants that** do not contribute a tremendous amount to our life and, if allowed to run riot, can stop our positive growth. **Digging up weeds** in a dream therefore shows that we are aware that by freeing our life of the non-essential, we are creating space for new growth.

WEEPING—*also see Mourning* Weeping suggests uncontrollable emotion or grief, so to experience either **ourselves or someone else weeping** is to show that there needs to be a discharge of such emotion. We may be sad over past events or fearful of moving into the future. It is worthwhile exploring the quality of weeping. For example, are we sobbing and therefore not able to express ourselves fully?

WEIGHING To be **weighing something** in dreams is to be assessing its worth. This image connects with the calculation of our needs and what is of value to us, whether materially or spiritually.

WEIGHT Experiencing a weight in a dream is to be conscious of our responsibilities. It may also suggest that we should assess the importance and seriousness of what we are doing.

WELCOME To **receive a welcome** in a dream suggests that we are accepting of our own selves. We are beginning to like who we are. If the welcome is from **a member of our family** we are being accepted by, and accepting, a better relationship with the family.

WELL A well is a way of assessing the deepest resources of emotion that we have. If there is something wrong with the well, e.g. we cannot reach the water, we are not able to get in touch with our best talents.

WHEEL A wheel in a dream indicates the ability and need to make changes to move forward into the future without being thrown off course.

WHIP The whip is an instrument of torture and indicates the dreamer has either the need to control others or to be controlled by them. We may be trying to control by using pain—either physical or emotional.

WHIRLPOOL / WHIRLWIND Both of these images are symbols of a vortex, a representation of life and natural energy. When they appear in dreams we are aware of the quality of power we have inside us. A whirlpool will probably represent emotional energy, whereas a whirlwind will suggest intellectual power.

WHISPERING—*also see Gossip* To **hear whispering** in a dream suggests that we need to listen to someone or something very carefully. It may also mean that we do not have the full information available to us about a situation in our waking life.

WHISTLE A whistle being blown in a dream can mark the end of a particular phase of time. It can also sound as a warning to alert us to a particular event.

WIDOW Dreaming about being a widow can suggest loss and sadness. Sometimes such a dream can mark the change in a woman's awareness as she moves onwards in age towards the "Crone" or Wise Woman. For a **woman to dream of a widow** highlights her ability to be free and use her own innate wisdom.

WIG In previous times, covering the head was considered to be a way of hiding the intellect, of giving a false impression or of indicating wisdom and authority. A **judge's wig** can suggest all of these. A **hairpiece or toupee** highlights false ideas or an unnatural attitude.

WILD In dreams anything wild always represents the untamed. Within each of us there is a part that dislikes being controlled in any way. It is the part of ourselves that needs to be free, and is creative and independent. A **wild animal** will stand for the aspect of our personality that has not yet committed itself to using rational thought.

WILL To dream about a will or any legal document is connected with the way in which our unconscious side can push us into taking notice of our inner needs. To be **making a will** is to be making a promise to ourselves over future action. It may also have overtones of attempting to look after those we love and care about. To **inherit from a will** in a dream means that we need to look at the habits, characteristics and morals we have inherited from our ancestors.

WIND In dreams, the wind symbolizes the intellect. It will depend on the force of the wind how we interpret the dream. For instance, **a breeze** would suggest gentleness and pleasure. An idea or concept we have is beginning to move us. **A gale or hurricane** might indicate a principle we feel passionately about or that we are being buffeted by circumstances beyond our control so need to take shelter. A **north wind** might suggest a threat to our security.

WINDMILL The image of a windmill in dreams can often suggest the correct use of resources. Because wind often suggests intellect, it is therefore the use of intellectual assets.

WINE—*also see Alcohol* In dreams, wine can suggest a happy occasion. As a substance it has an influence on our awareness and appreciation of our environment. A **wine cellar**, therefore, can represent the sum of our past experiences, both good and bad. A **wine bottle**, as a source of enjoyment, is taken by some to indicate masculinity.

WINGS Because wings make us think of flight, to dream about, for instance, **birds' wings** would suggest attention is being drawn to our need for freedom. A **broken wing** indicates that a previous trauma is preventing us from "taking off."

WINTER In dreams, winter can represent an unfruitful time in our life . It can also represent old age—a time when our energy is running down.

WISDOM To dream that we are wise indicates the potential we have to run our life successfully and to relate meaningfully to other people.

WITNESS When we find ourselves in the position of **being a witness** to, for instance, an accident, it may be that our powers of observation are being highlighted. We need to take careful note of what is going on around us. Our interaction with authority may also be being called into question.

WOOD—*also see Forest, Plank and Trees* Dreaming about wood, in the sense of timber, suggests our ability to appreciate the past and to build on what has gone before. We are capable of building a structure, which may or may not be permanent. Dreaming about **a wooden toy** highlights our connection with the more natural side of ourselves.

WOOL How we interpret wool depends on whether the image we have is of lamb's wool or of knitting wool *(see Knitting)*. **Lamb's wool** may stand for blurred thoughts and feelings that we have not yet figured out.

WORD When in dreams we are conscious of a word being repeated, it can be either the sound or the meaning that is significant.

WORK Dreaming about being at work highlights issues, concerns or difficulties that we may need to address within our work situation.

WORKSHOP In dreams a workshop symbolizes the part of ourselves that creates projects which are beneficial to us, although not necessarily financially.

WORM At its very basic interpretation, the worm can suggest the penis. Depending on the dreamer's attitude to sexuality and gender, there may be a sense of threat.

WORSHIP—*also see Religious Imagery* Dreaming about being in a situation where we are **worshiping something,** such as an idea, a person, a concept or an object, is to be opening ourselves up to its influence. If we are not particularly religious but find ourselves in the middle of **an act of worship**, we may need to look at how we deal with a common belief system.

WOUND—*also see Weapon* Any wound or trauma in dreams signifies hurt feelings or emotions. **If we are inflicting the wounds**, our own aggression and mistrust are being highlighted. **If the wounds are being inflicted on us**, we may be making ourselves into, or being, the victim.

WREATH A wreath in a dream can suggest honor. A circular shape signifies continuity and completeness, as well as everlasting life. **Dreaming about being given a wreath** suggests being singled out, perhaps for some honor, although it was formerly believed to warn of potential death. **Dreaming about giving someone else a wreath** validates our relationship with that person.

WRECK Dreaming about a wreck—such as a **car or shipwreck**—indicates that our plans may be thwarted in some way. It is necessary to decide whether we are at fault for the failure of our plans or someone or something else is.

WRITING To dream about writing is an attempt to communicate information that one has. Sometimes **the instrument we are writing** with is important. For instance, **a pencil** would suggest that the information is less permanent than with **a pen**, whereas a **typewriter or word processor** would tend to suggest business communication rather than personal.

X,Y,Z: X to Zoo

X If an X appears in a dream, we are usually "marking the spot." It can also represent an error, a misjudgment or possibly something that we particularly need to note.

X RAYS Dreaming about X-rays can mean that there is something influencing the dreamer's life on an unconscious level that needs to be revealed. **If the dreamer is carrying out the X-ray** it may be necessary to look more deeply into a situation. There may also be a fear of illness, either in oneself or others.

YARN Yarn in the sense of knitting yarn or twine often signifies our ability to create order out of chaos. In olden times it suggested spinning, an archetypal symbol for life, and often in dreams it is this image that is portrayed. We fashion our life out of what we are given.

YAWN If we become conscious of yawning in a dream it can indicate boredom and tiredness. We may also be attempting to say something, but have not yet thought through what we wish to say.

YEARNING Feelings in dreams are often heightened in intensity. A sense of yearning in a dream would highlight an emotion that we need to look at more closely in order to understand.

YEAST Yeast is accepted as a substance that both lightens food and makes it palatable. At the same time, it changes the substance and texture. In dreams it represents ideas or influences that can irrevocably change our life or situations, often for the better.

YES Occasionally in dreams we become aware that we have 'said' yes. This is an instinctive acceptance or acknowledgment of whatever has been happening.

YIELD To yield in a dream is to be aware of the futility of confrontation. To understand this, we may need to look at particular situations in our life.

YIN YANG With its origins in Chinese philosophy, this symbol represents the balance of two opposite but complementary energies. In dreams it indicates the balance between the instinctive, intuitive nature of the feminine and the active, rational nature of the masculine.

ZIGZAG When we see a zigzag in dreams we are looking at the potential to be hit by disaster, such as a bolt of lightning—an event that will bring about a great discharge of energy. Circumstances will then be brought back into balance.

ZIP A zip appearing in a dream may indicate our ability—or difficulty—in maintaining relationships with other people. A stuck zip suggests a difficulty in keeping our dignity in an awkward situation.

ZOO Dreaming about being in a zoo suggests the need to understand some of our natural urges and instincts. We perhaps need to be more objective in our appraisal of them than we have been up until now.